STUCK ON AN ISLAND

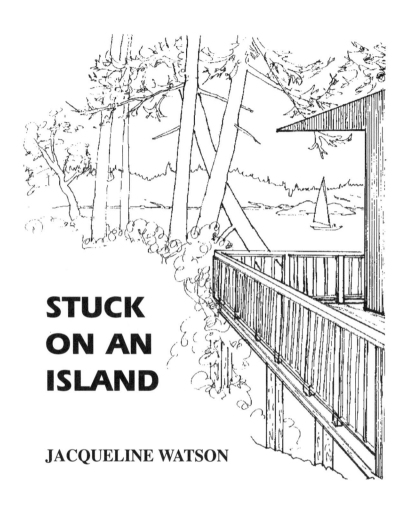

STUCK
ON AN
ISLAND

JACQUELINE WATSON

ILLUSTRATIONS BY MIGS RUSSELL EDWARDS

J. Books, Publisher
125 Marina Crescent Drive
Salt Spring Island
B.C., Canada V8K 2R2

755 Rosecrans Street
San Diego, CA 92106
U.S.A.

Cover painting and chapter illustrations copyright © Migs Russell Edwards

Design and typesetting by Cooper-Wood Graphics, San Diego, CA.

Printed in Canada by Hignell Book Printing Limited, 488 Burnell Street, Winnipeg, Manitoba, Canada R3G 2B4.

Words from *The Elders Are Watching* by David Bouchard are reproduced by permission of the author and the publisher, Raincoast Books 8680 Cambie Street, Vancouver, B.C. Canada V6P 6M9

First printing 1997
Second printing, revised 1998

Canadian Cataloguing in Publication Data
Watson, Jacqueline, 1932-
  Stuck on an island

ISBN 0-9683081-0-4

1. Watson, Jacqueline, 1932- 2. Saltspring Island (B.C.)--
Biography. 3. Saltspring Island (B.C.)--History. I. Edward.
Migs Russell, 1920- II. Title.
FC3845.S27Z49 1998   971.1'2804'092   C97-911038-6
F1089.S2W37 1998

Dedicated to Maurie, Scott and Charlotte,
with happy memories

The settings, events and characters in this book
are real; however, there is a touch of poetic license
and some names are fictionalized.

ACKNOWLEDGEMENTS

I thank the many people who helped me write this book: Maurice Watson, my husband, for his editing and his loving support; Michael Grant of San Diego for being my mentor and editor for three years; Migs Russell Edwards for the illustrating the book and for her assistance with island and Maracaibo history; Sue Diaz, for her encouragement and advice; The First Sunday Writing Group of San Diego for their comments and corrections during the last six years; Robin Cooper-Wood for computer design; Ivan and Sue Mouat for the Mouat family history; Frank Richards for his advice and papers on the sewer controversy; Tom Toynbee for background of Mouat's Trading Company; Mary Davidson, Archivist for the Archives of Salt Spring Historical Society; Hank Schubart for his recollection of island development and his vision for the future.

I thank the many islanders who assisted with information: Jim Ballantyne, Archie and Kas Black, Allen, Cyril and Carrie Louise Cunningham, Loes Holland, Gundy and Ann McLeod, Mary Moat, Dennis and Carol Scott, Thea Van Meel.

I want to acknowledge the following sources from which I've gleaned ideas and information: *Mouat Family Centennial History, Salt Spring Island, 1885-1985; Salt Spring Island, British Columbia, 1895* by Reverend C.F. Wilson; *Salt Spring Island* by Bea Hamilton; *Gunkholing in the San Juans* by Al Cummings and Jo Bailey Cummings; *The Gulf Islanders Explorer: The Outdoor Guide* by Bruce Obee; *Exploring South Coast of British Columbia* by Don Douglas and Renee Hemingway-Douglas; *An Explorer's Guide: Marine Parks of British Columbia* by Peter Chettleburgh; *Once Upon An Island* by David Conover; *Snow Falling On Cedars* by David Guterson; *Gift of the Sea* by Anne Morrow Lindbergh; *Gulf Islands. 1976 Edition* by Bill Wolferson; *"A Voice From the Past"* by Tom Wright appearing in *Gulf Islands Guardian Magazine; Gulf Islands Driftwood; The Victoria Times; The Gulf Islander* guide; B.C. Ferries *Advancing the Fleet/ Building the Province* brochure; *The Elders Are Watching* by David Bouchard and Roy Henry Vickers; "Salt Spring Island: Star of the Gulf Islands" by Jeremy J.P. Moray.

CONTENTS

1

STUCK ON AN ISLAND

The gray, rocky shores quietly appeared in the fog. I stood on the deck, squinting to see the harbour, the haze moistening my face and my hair. Trees emerged like sentinels along the shoreline. The ferry terminal gradually appeared through the scrim. My excitement rose. I dashed downstairs to the car deck where Maurie, my husband, was waiting in our station wagon. I flung the car door open and announced, "The ferry's going to dock!"

At the end of the open car deck, a sign, *Long Harbour, Salt Spring Island,* appeared in the mist. The ferry noisily attached itself to the terminal landing.

Lanes of cars were waiting to board and take our places; foot passengers quickly walked to the terminal; islanders waited for friends or family to arrive; streams of cyclists undulated up Long Harbour Road toward the village of Ganges. Our station wagon and U-Haul trailer clanged down the ramp in line with other cars but broke ranks upon reaching land and turned left toward Scott Point.

Arbutus trees sporting white blossoms of spring and tender-green branch tips of Douglas fir, balsam and cedar trees edged the road. Like hesitant debutantes, the dogwood trees were just beginning to blossom. At a fork in the road, pointing to the left, stood the sign: *Marina Crescent Drive.* Our wagon took the left fork. I breathed deeply...and wished that everything was going to be all right. It had been such a long journey up the coast from San Diego.

We passed one house before turning into a driveway draped with verdant leaves of overhanging maple trees. There stood a modern, split-level house with two carports and a storage shed. The underbrush, full of salal, salmonberry, sword ferns, red huckleberry and spaghnum moss, made a resplendent carpet beneath the trees. A light March rain began to fall, coating everything in crystal brilliance.

The house, painted a muted olive-green, blended with the fir and cedar trees standing quietly by. We walked along the wet top deck to the back door. My heart pounded in my ears...louder than Maurie's fist pounding on the door. A man, cradling a pipe in his hand, opened the door and said, "You must be the Watsons."

"Are you Mr. Lawson?" Maurie asked.

"Yes, I'm Jim Lawson. Come in."

The aromatic scent from the cedar walls was an elixir to my senses. My eyes widened with the panoramic view of the harbour framed by cathedral windows. An inviting fire burned in the corner brick fireplace; the chimney smoke curled outside the window and dissipated into the mist. The warmth of the room gave the feeling of snug coziness. Relief rose within me. *Yes, we have done the right thing.*

"I'm glad you made it all the way up here. That was a long trip from San Diego," Lawson said.

"Yeah, 1,400 miles pulling a U-Haul trailer full of furniture isn't the easiest," Maurie replied. He paused and glanced at Lawson, "I'm a little confused. Are you the owner?"

"Yes, indeed, I am," Lawson answered. "I am also the realtor--that is, my wife owns this house and I'm handling the deal for her."

"I see," Maurie said with a puzzled look on his face. I sensed something was not quite right.

"Excuse me, I didn't introduce my friend." Jim Lawson turned toward the fireplace and pointed. There sat a little man with straw-like hair and strange eyes. "This is the Beachcomber. We call him that because he's always picking up driftwood and odd things from the shore in his boat."

The Beachcomber stared at us, not moving. I felt uneasy. Who *is this* guy? "Glad to meet ya," he said. Then he frowned and blurted out, "So, you folks got stuck on this island, eh?"

I looked at this creature, wondering what he meant, and what he was doing in the house. Lawson laughed, probably from uneasiness of his own. Had he stuck us with this house? Maurie shut his eyes, dismissed the comment and said, "I thought we'd move our furniture into the house as soon as possible."

Lawson's face grew dark. His voice had a hesitant tone. "I'm sorry to disappoint you, Mr. and Mrs. Watson, but since the title for the house will not change hands and be legally yours until April 1, I can't allow you to bring your furnishings in here."

"What difference does that make? It's just a matter of a few days before the house is ours." An edge of irritation rose in Maurie's voice.

"You knew we were coming up with a trailer-load of furniture. Why didn't you tell us beforehand that we couldn't store things here?" I asked, wondering if Lawson was going by some Canadian law at the last minute.

"Ha-ha! Folks, this island ain't easy," the Beachcomber cackled, happy over our problem.

A heavy pause hung above us. Rings of pipe smoke drifted into the air. In a condescending tone, Lawson said, "All right. I guess you can store everything on the lower level until the house is legally yours."

I was angry that the beauty of the moment was ruined by this ornery so-and-so. I turned on my heel, "Come on, Maurie, let's get this stuff unloaded." Under my breath, I muttered, *What a pain in the butt, storing everything down below.*

The Beachcomber leaned over the railing on the top deck; he watched us unload every armful from the U-Haul trailer. His wild eyes examined our belongings as if he were putting price tags on them. We marched down the stairs with the wet furniture and marched up the stairs under the gaze of that weird little man. Maurie was quiet; his expression was grim. I felt wet, tired and disheartened. It took us an hour to unload. We left, not saying goodbye to Jim Lawson.

We drove back in silence to the Long Harbour terminal to catch the afternoon ferry to the Tsawwassen, a mainland terminal located 40 kilometers south of Vancouver. Windshield wipers worked furiously as rain pelted the window. The dirt road was a slippery mess.

"That Jim Lawson thinks he's as slick as this road," Maurie finally said.

"What do you mean?" I asked.

"I don't trust that bugger, but he's not as smart as he thinks he is."

"I don't understand what you're saying."

"He rejected my all cash offer in exchange for a small reduction on the purchase price."

"So?"

"He'll lose a lot more in purchasing power over the next ten years, which is the mortgage period, because of inflation. We'll get a much bigger reduction. Dumb."

"He deserves it after the way he acted."

"I still have misgivings about buying a house way up here. What happened today makes me even more edgy."

Second thoughts about the house flooded my mind. My throat tightened. I gazed out the window into the rainy woods, remembering how we first discovered the island on our summer vacation to Canada, how its beauty and separateness enamored me, how I wanted a house on Long Harbour and found one and how excited we were to successfully negotiate the purchase of the house. I recalled proudly announcing the news of our acquisition to friends and family and their reactions coming back at us:

"You what?"

"You bought a summer house? On an island? In Canada? 1,400 miles away?"

"How are you going to furnish it?"

"Why didn't you buy something closer to home in San Diego?"

"Can you afford to use it only in the summertime?"

"How did you ever find the island?"

The rain poured. I looked at my unhappy husband and wondered if buying the house was the right decision after all. The rain-swept road ahead was as obscured as the paths, the human entanglements and the troubles that awaited us.

2

A FATEFUL VACATION

It was an accident. That's how we discovered our house on the island. Simply by accident. It was over twenty years ago. Maurie was forty-seven years old and I was thirty-nine. Our son, Scott, was ten and daughter, Charlotte, was just six. We lived in a redwood home overlooking a San Diego canyon. One night at the dinner table, Maurie said, "Why don't we rent a motor home this summer and take the kids up the West Coast, maybe go as far as Canada. I've always wanted to travel in an R.V."

"Yah, yah, Dad," encouraged our two kids. "That would be neat. We can see mountains...and trees." they said with excitement.

"That would be fun." I was already thinking about taking our two nieces. "How many would an R.V. sleep?" I asked.

"I think six people, max."

"What would you think about taking Lynn and Julie? They don't get to go many places." How foolish I was then. It never occurred to me what work it might be—cooped up for three weeks with two kids and two nieces in a tin can on wheels.

"Well, that would be a nice thing to do for them," Maurie said. "Let's think about it. I'll check around about R.V. rentals."

The summer of 1970 drew near. In June we made the decision to go on our vacation to the Northwest. Maurie found a Winnebago we could rent from two lawyer-friends during the month of August...and at a bargain. We invited Lynn and Julie to join us; they were thrilled at the prospect of traveling. Their mother was dead and their father couldn't afford vacations.

I had great fun plotting and planning our trip with the kids. I gathered games, coloring books, crayons and cards to keep them amused. For weeks I stocked up on canned goods and staples to feed six people.

An old photograph shows us loading the R.V. There was Maurie, my attorney-husband, who looked like a professional even wearing a white t-shirt and khaki shorts; strangers often asked him if he was a doctor. His broad intelligent face, his brown hair neatly clipped in a crew cut and his sharp brown eyes framed by tortoiseshell glasses gave him an air of wisdom. And he *was* wise. Forever reading, forever storing information in his brain. Quiet and analytical by nature, he was a trusted counselor to many, but most of all to me.

Perhaps going to Canada was a subliminal, sentimental journey for Maurie. His father, Jack, was taken from England by his grandmother at the age of eleven to live near Toronto. Jack later served in the Canadian army during World War I. While on leave in London, he met Maurie's mother, May, who was a twenty-one year old Londoner. After their meeting, Jack romanced her by letter. When the war ended, May came by ship to marry Jack in Canada. The family immigrated from Toronto to San Diego in the 1920's with little money. Modest upbringing made Maurie a cautious, conservative man. Forever British in their hearts, the family raised Maurie and his three siblings to take pride in their English heritage.

Maurie physically stood out in a crowd—he was six feet, four inches tall and slim—but was periodically plagued by back trouble resulting from tuberculosis of the bone followed by surgery at the end of World War II. His ambition to become a dentist like his older brother was thwarted by his back, so he took advantage of the G.I. Bill, and directed his intellectual talents toward the law.

We met at Stanford University. Maurie was in his last year of law school and I was a graduate student working toward my masters degree and teaching credentials. He had a maturity about him; the war and his illness had leavened him. He studied hard in law school, earned the respect of his fellow students and received the honor of serving on the board of editors for the Stanford Law Review. These qualities were attractive to me, so our love affair blossomed that year. After graduation, he encouraged me to teach in San Diego. The following year, when he passed the bar, we decided to marry. I was teaching speech and drama at La Jolla Junior-Senior High School when we were married. He became a partner practicing law with a small, respected San Diego firm specializing in taxes, business and estate planning.

We had been married sixteen years that summer when we launched our rented motor home for Canada. Maurie looked like the captain at the helm of a ship as he drove north toward San Francisco. I glanced back at the kids from my seat. There were smiles on their faces. Scott wore dark-rimmed glasses, a blue T-shirt and checkered shorts, wiggling with excitement. Our dainty daughter, Charlotte, sat primly in her flowered shift smoothing back wisps of blonde hair falling in her face. Lynn, our lanky eleven-year-old niece, cuddled next to her sister Julie, a teenager on the brink of womanhood.

The bargain rental proved not to be such a bargain. The air-conditioner quit in the heat of the hot San Joaquin Valley. The quirky R.V. battery didn't have enough juice to start the motor, so we bought a second battery and attached it from the outside with jumper cables to the battery under the hood, just to get going each time. There was a long, deep shelf that dropped down over the driver's seat and it was the only place large enough for Maurie to sleep. My bed was a sleeping bag on top of the collapsed kitchen table. The four kids squashed into bunk beds in the rear of the R.V.

Clothes and cans, crammed into every corner, came tumbling down with any sudden stop.

"I've made reservations at an R.V. park in Redwood City," Maurie shouted over the hum of the motor. "Let's pull in and get cleaned up. Then we'll take the kids to that great Basque restaurant in San Francisco." The R.V. windows were open to catch the warm winds of San Joaquin Valley; our hot, sweaty faces brightened at the thought of dinner in cool San Francisco.

We stared, aghast, as we pulled the Winnebago into the R.V. park in Redwood City. It was a tumbled down establishment with weeds lining the driveway, rusty electrical lines and leaky water connections at the parking space.

"Yuk! This place is the pits," complained the kids.

"I must agree, it's pretty awful," I said.

"Christ! This isn't what I expected." Maurie looked disgusted. "Let's take a shower and get outta here. We can park the bus on a quiet street in San Francisco and spend the night." The park's shower stall was moldy and spit water everywhere, except on the body. We left in a hurry.

The quaint, family-style restaurant was a refreshing change from the run-down R.V. park. The plentiful food raised our spirits. We consumed a sumptuous dinner of a tureen of soup, a platter of fresh salad, bowls of steaming vegetables, huge slices of roast beef and ending with cakes and pies—perfect fare for a big family. Our stomachs felt full. We walked to the R.V. in the cool evening. Maurie moved the Winnebago and parked it on a dark street a few blocks away from the Broadway tunnel...slightly on an uphill angle.

Everyone bedded down, except Lynn who was dawdling in the bathroom. Suddenly she cried, "Help, Auntie Jackie, help!" I jumped out of my sleeping bag and reached the door in two strides. "The toilet has overflowed and it's all over the floor! What should I do?" I looked at the floor. "It's just water that's overflowed, Lynn. Please get out of the here, so I can clean it up." I knew Lynn flustered easily and that Julie would help. "Everybody out! Julie, stay with me and help sop up this water." In a moment everyone was clustered outside the doorway.

"The bus is on a tilt—that's why the water spilled over." Maurie yelled from outside. "I know where to pull the plug and let the water out. No problem!"

Julie and I were cleaning the bathroom floor with sponges when we heard Maurie shout, "Oh, my God, I pulled the wrong plug!"

We scrambled out the door and stood in our pajamas watching the dark contents of the holding tank flow down the streets of San Francisco. Maurie stood looking helplessly at the unsavory plug in his hand.

"It stinks out here!" Scott shouted and held his nose.

"Not so loud, Scott." I whispered. "Let's go before we're arrested for polluting the street. Everybody back into the RV." We were like a Chinese fire drill clamoring into the Winnebago.

Maurie angrily replaced the plug, upset with himself, knowing his lawyering abilities far exceeded his mechanical abilities. He turned on the motor and gunned it furiously. We roared away into the night. The kids and I, holding our sides with laughter, looked out the back window at the brown, dribbling trail in the street. "We left our 'harumph' instead of our hearts in San Francisco," I said with tears in my eyes. We had no choice but to return to Redwood City. Maurie parked the Winnebago in its shabby space, took a couple of strong swigs of Scotch and crawled up on his shelf to sleep away his mechanical frustrations.

I was dozing off when Charlotte's little voice asked in the night, "Mommie, what's 'harumph'?"

Along with the flooding came a feast of new experiences. I watched the children stand in awe of huge, towering redwoods; they were fascinated with high-powered water stripping bark from logs in a lumber mill; they picked and ate buckets of blackberries; they played in quiet coves and lush rain forests; they heard the roar of glacial waters; they hiked in the shadows of snow-capped mountains.

Our northern-most stop was Victoria, British Columbia. We rode a double decker bus, dined on seafood and sipped tea at the famed Empress Hotel. At the end of a delightfully warm day, we hooked up the R.V. in a cool, tree-shaded park near the city.

I had an idea. "Maurie, why don't we ask Julie to baby-sit while we go out to dinner? I noticed a Victorian restaurant just down the street and we can walk to it," I suggested.

Maurie smiled. "Good idea, Jacque." "Jacque" was his nickname for me and a good indication he was in a receptive mood. "You've cooked for six of us two weeks straight. Let's ask her."

"Sure, Auntie Jackie, I'll take care of the kids," Julie said. "You guys go and have a good time."

We strolled down the tree-lined street to a charming restaurant and enjoyed a quiet dinner without being interrupted by a child; it was the most relaxing evening we had in two weeks. We walked slowly back in the moonlight, arm in arm, and quietly stepped into the bus. Everyone was asleep. All was calm. Maurie put his arms around me, held me close and gave me a long goodnight kiss. I wanted to climb up on the shelf with him, but there was no room. I snuggled into my sleeping bag, feeling wonderful.

Suddenly the Winnebago began to vibrate. A gushing, churning sound pounded from the rear of the R.V. I jumped out of the bag and the moment I put my feet in the aisle, I felt water rushing between my toes.

"Christ, sounds like something blew!" Maurie exclaimed. He jumped off his shelf and ran outside in his skivvies. "It might be the water pump. I'll turn off the water connection."

We sponged and mopped for over an hour to sop up water from the floor. The kids never woke up. I wearily crawled back into my sleeping bag. In the dark came Maurie's whisper, "Welcome back to your pumpkin, Cinderella!"

After Victoria, we drove to Swartz Bay to take a ferry back to the mainland. Maurie said, "I just thought of something. I've got a client, Jack Russell, who is retired on one of the islands somewhere between Victoria and Vancouver. Why don't I try to look him up in the phone directory, and if I find him, let's stop on his island?"

"Sounds like a good idea," I said, "it should be beautiful on those islands. We can pay him a visit tomorrow morning."

We found a phone booth, parked the R.V. next to it and Maurie located Jack Russell in the phone book. He dialed the number and the conversation went like this:

"No, Dad isn't here. I'm Jim, his son. Dad and Mom are at the neighbour's playing bridge."

"Can you get him for me? I'm calling from Victoria."

"Sorry. I can't. The neighbour lives a half mile away."

"I see. We're friends of his from San Diego. We're in a motor home and we thought of taking a ferry to your island on our return to Vancouver. Is there a park on your island where we could park the motor home—then we could see your dad in the morning?"

"Yah, there's Mouat's Provincial Park. Come on over and I'll tell him you're on your way. When you get to the village—it's called Ganges—give us another call."

The small ferry crossed the calm waters at sunset. The unknown island loomed before us. It was lush with heavy growth. The paved road from the ferry terminal looped by farms, herds of sheep, apple trees, vistas of coves and hills of trees. It was dark when we arrived in the village, but we found a telephone booth and again called Jack.

"Where are you?" I could hear Jack's voice ask as I stood cramped in the telephone booth with Maurie. "We're in Ganges...in a phone booth next to some store." Maurie answered. "Stay there. I know just where you are because there's only one phone booth in the village." Jack Russell soon pulled up in his car. "Hello, Maurie, glad to see you," he said with a broad smile. "What a nice surprise!" "Hello, Jack. Hope you don't mind our coming in on you on the spur of the moment. I'd like you to meet my wife, Jackie." "So nice to meet you, Jack," I said. "This is our niece, Julie. The other three kids are asleep in the R.V." I estimated Jack to be in his fifties. His dark hair was streaked with gray. He stood tall wearing dark-rimmed glasses.

"Get back in your R.V. and follow me to the house," Jack said. "You can park in my driveway for the night. Jackie, come with me in my car."

I wondered where Jack was taking us in the black of night. His car bumped over a dusty road which disappeared into the dark forest. The R.V. lights danced behind us. Overhanging boughs and branches attacked and scraped the car roof. *What are we getting into?* I wondered to myself.

3

GETTING TO KNOW THE ISLAND

"Salt Spring is the name of our island," Jack said, driving along. "It's the largest of the Gulf Islands." The dash lights reflecting on his face showed a friendly smile that put me at ease. "We lie roughly 68 kilometers northwest of Victoria and about 100 kilometers west of Vancouver."

"Why is the island called Salt Spring?"

"Because there are salt springs bubbling up out of the ground toward the north end of the island." He spoke proudly of the island. "We have a summer cottage located at the end of a harbour called Long Harbour. Long Harbour lies northeast of the central part of the island so that's why it's a bit of a drive. I invested in a peninsula along the north side of the harbour several years ago which included the cottage. Now my family and I live up here year round."

"Since you live up here, how is it that Maurie is your lawyer?"

"Well, we used to live in Del Mar. I still own vineyards in Borrego Springs and property in San Diego. I needed legal help and Maurie's firm was recommended to me. I've been working with him ever since."

House lights appeared in the black night, outlining two figures waiting on the back deck. "There's my wife, Migs, and Jim," Jack said. "Janet's my daughter but she's gone right now."

I felt uncomfortable again—coming in on strangers late at night and parking in their driveway.

"Hello. I'm Migs Russell." A pretty woman with auburn hair extended her hand to me. "You must be Maurie's wife." Piercing blue eyes looked me over. "Welcome to Salt Spring."

"Hi, I'm Jackie. I hope we're not imposing on you this late at night." I said.

"Not at all. Come in for a drink."

I remember Migs rocked in her chair in front of a view window, looked out into the pitch black and told us about the island. Her colourful descriptions left me eager to see the dark isle in the daytime. We finished our drinks and said goodnight.

In the R.V., I said, "I don't want to trouble the Russells tomorrow. Let's keep the curtains closed until we've had breakfast and clean things up."

I was awake with the early morning light, dying of curiosity, full of excitement. I peeked through the closed curtains and couldn't believe the beautiful sight outside. A mill pond of blue-green water lay before my eyes; the rising sun ignited shafts of golden light on the water. One or two pleasure boats floated lazily at anchor. Around the harbour's edge the dark reflection of cedar trees and Douglas firs undulated with the slightest ripple of water. Brilliantly orange arbutus trees and Garry oaks were sprinkled among the lush green forest. A few cabins were tucked among trees on the opposite shore. An azure blue sky was a backdrop for the idyllic scene. *What a gorgeous sight! I think I'm going to like this place.* Then I got excited. *I wish everyone would wake up so I can get out and really see everything.* I patiently lay in my sleeping bag for an hour and then my excitement got the best me. "Everybody up and at'em," I said. "We've got lots of things to do and see today, so let's get going."

I wouldn't let anybody out until everything was cleaned up and everyone had on clean clothes. After about forty-five minutes, Jack's voice called from outside.

"Hello in there. Anybody up?" We opened the door and stepped outside. "Why don't you come in for a cup of coffee," Jack said, "then I'll take everyone for a boat ride to see Long Harbour."

Before we knew it, we were in Jack's eighteen-foot, inboard runabout smoothly slicing through the protected waters of the fjord-like harbour. A small private resort called Maracaibo lay adjacent to Jack's property; it consisted of a clubhouse, three A-frame cottages, a swimming pond, and an open field. The rest of the peninsula on the north side was Jack's—it looked pure and pristine. The Long Harbour ferry terminal with its massive pilings and its modest waiting room came into view on the south shore. "That's where you'll be boarding the ferry this afternoon," Jack told us. Across from the terminal, a tall fragment of an island with sparse bushes and straggly trees stood midstream in the harbour. A few minutes beyond the ferry landing appeared a private marina with some docks and yachts. An occasional house or cabin dotted the south shore.

Jack stopped the motor at the mouth of the harbour and the boat bobbed quietly with the incoming tide. Seagulls called overhead. The deep moan of a ferry horn echoed in the distance. On the horizon a ferry appeared to move as if in slow motion. The salt air filled my lungs. A gentle summer wind brushed my face. My total being was caught up in the beauty of the surroundings; I felt one with nature.

"The end of my peninsula is called Nose Point," Jack gestured as he talked. "That white marker with its blinking light guides the ferry into the harbour at night and during bad weather. See the ol' carved wooden sea captain standing on the other side of the harbour? That's called Scott Point. The owner of the house at the end of the point is from Newport Beach and he always puts the captain out by the flagpole to let people know when he and his wife are up from California."

The ride was too short. I only saw a bit of the island and that was beautiful. I wanted to see more. My appetite was whetted, but time ran out. We had to catch the 1:30 P.M. ferry to the Tsawwassen terminal.

"We appreciate your hospitality, Jack," Maurie said and shook Jack's hand. "Thanks for the boat ride."

"You're welcome," Jack said.

"Long Harbour is a beautiful spot and I hate to leave," I called out from the R.V. "Perhaps someday we can come back." I waved goodbye to the Russells as the motor home turned toward the road leading to the ferry terminal.

The beautiful scenes were already etched in memory. Salt Spring Island had hooked my heart. *Someday,* I vowed inwardly, *we will come back.*

Memories of Salt Spring Island kept bubbling on the back burner of my brain. I shared our Northwest adventures with friends and family and always concluded my stories with the discovery of the island. Our summer vacation in 1971 was spent in Europe while Maurie attended the American Bar Convention in London. I enjoyed Europe but the yearning to return to the island stayed with me

When it was time to start planning our vacation for the summer of '72, I asked Maurie, "What would you think about returning to Salt Spring Island with our kids this summer?"

"Good idea, Jacque. Let's take our motorboat up there too." Maurie said. "Maybe I'll call Jack Russell and see if we can rent an A-frame cottage at Maracaibo."

One evening Maurie came home from the office, saying, "I called Jack about Maracaibo and he said only members can stay in the cottages. However, he thinks there's a downstairs apartment that's available—it's across the harbour from him."

"Oh, I hope it is. I really want to go back there and spend some time."

In a couple of days, Jack called our home. "I've made arrangements for you to stay at the neighbour's apartment in August."

"That's wonderful, Jack," I said, "I'll tell Maurie and we'll start making our plans."

"We're looking forward to seeing you again. You'll like our neighbours and their apartment. Their last name is Cunningham. You'll be able to hop in your boat and come across the harbour to see us."

It's amazing how new friends enter your life, particularly when you're not looking for them. Perhaps that's what serendipity is all about...finding good friends accidentally. I had no idea when I first met Cyril and Carrie Louise Cunningham what true and lasting friends they would become.

Cyril, with his cheery face and twinkling blue eyes, captured my heart from the beginning. His full head of closely cropped white hair gave him a boyish look even though he was in his seventies. His parents were both British which explained his fair English complexion and gentlemanly ways.

"We're pleased to have you stay with us," Cyril said. "You can launch your boat at the end of the road, then tie it up to our dock." Cyril was short in stature but he was strong in body. He had a limp from a previous knee injury which he ignored. We discovered that he was in perpetual motion from dawn to dusk climbing up and down ladders, repairing wells—he always had several projects under way at the same time.

Life on the prairies started him off as a hearty soul. "I was born in what is now the Canadian province of Saskatchewan on the coldest day in January of 1900," he once told us. "My family moved to small-town Victoria which was growing fast then. When I was nine years old, I watched the Empress Hotel rise on pilings driven into a slough, which is now Victoria Inner Harbour. Then I left British Columbia as a young man and studied entomology with my uncle in New Orleans. It was there I met Carrie Louise."

"Yes, sir," Carrie Louise added, "poor Cyril could see me only after playin' a game of checkers with Father. He played more checkers that year than anytime in his life. But, I was nineteen years old and it was the southern custom to be chaperoned. I think Father let me marry Cyril because he was such a good checkers player."

"It was a bit difficult for Carrie Louise to adjust to Vancouver after we were married," Cyril told us.

"Livin' up north was soooo different from the south," Carrie Louise drawled. "I missed my Mammy who always took care of me. Vancouver was cold and windy. Couldn't sit in your rockin' chair on the front porch like you could in New Orleans. I nearly froze to death that first year. I was used to eatin' southern cookin' instead of drinkin' tea and nibblin' scones. Oh, how I missed Mother and New Orleans."

Carrie Louise was the same height as Cyril. Her black, curly hair framed an olive complexion and her deep brown eyes hinted of French background. She moved in slower motion than Cyril and often said, "Hurryin' is for Yankees." There was always a poodle on her lap or in her arms.

"How did you two get to Salt Spring from Vancouver?" I asked.

"When Cyril turned sixty-five and retired, we bought property on the island at the end of Long Harbour thinkin' it'd be a nice retirement spot." Carrie Louise replied. "However, I didn't know we would become 'pioneers' livin' in a trailer with all the hardships of buildin' a house. Thank goodness Allen, that's our son, came weekends and summers to help us build. Bless his heart, he's a teacher and a bachelor and had plenty of time."

The many kindnesses shown us by the Russells and the Cunninghams made us feel right at home on the island. Jack took Maurie and Scott cod fishing in his boat. Migs brought an empty battery jar to the children for a salt water aquarium. "Find hermit crabs in abandoned shells, oysters from the shore and sea cucumbers," she said. "Put them in the jar, then drop in sea weed for atmosphere and you can watch all the activity." Carrie Louise and Cyril invited us and the Russells many times for drinks on their upstairs deck.

Days drifted by with new experiences, particularly for Scott and Charlotte: they pried oysters from rocks along the shore, collected shells and driftwood and caught crab in the Cunninghams' trap.

We discovered the island lay on a northwesterly axis with an irregular shape carved thousands of years ago by glaciers, melt water and seismic formations; it was twenty miles in length and varied from two to seven miles in width. Seventy-seven miles of coves, inlets and rocky shores edged the perimeter. Mountains were scattered across the island—Mt. Maxwell being the prominent one with a provincial park overlooking Fulford Harbour and the low-lying, distant San Juan Islands. Several lakes, such as St. Mary, Cusheon, Maxwell and Weston, provided water supply for surrounding areas; a variety of accommodations on some of the lakes attracted tourists and fishermen.

Ganges Harbour, the largest harbour on the island, was located southwest of Long Harbour. At the head of this harbour was a small village called Ganges, named for the 84-gun Royal Navy ship, H.M.S. Ganges, which was the last British sailing ship to patrol the surrounding waters in the late 1850s. A string of small scenic islands called the Chain Islands greeted boaters on their approach into Ganges.

In the village we found the phone booth where we first called Jack; it was next to a two-story general store called Mouat's. The imposing white building with dark green trim sold everything from fishing tackle, lumber and hardware downstairs to kitchenware, clothing and linens upstairs. Cyril worked in the hardware department a couple of days a week and told us Mouat's was one of the oldest stores in Ganges.

"Have you been in the Trading Post yet?" Cyril asked. "It's another old building in the village at the corner of McPhillips and Lower Ganges Roads. It was built the same year as Mouat's in 1912. The two stores used to be great competitors, but the Trading Post only sells groceries now."

A fuel dock, a government dock (always painted red), a boatyard and two marinas were located beyond Mouat's on the easterly side of the harbour. Green storage tanks stood on wooded Grace Point which jutted seaward below Mouat's, dividing Ganges Harbour. The western section of the harbour included a breakwater extending from Grace Point which protected a government dock, a boat basin, a boat ramp, and the waterfront Centennial Park.

Fulford-Ganges Road started in front of Mouat's, ran parallel with Centennial Park through the village and continued down-island to Fulford Harbour. As we walked along the road, we found the post office, a bank, a realty office, the volunteer fire station, a pharmacy and small shops.

The K&R Grocery Store, surrounded with ample parking, stood behind the bank and post office. Lower Ganges Road travelled northwest by the pharmacy and gas station, The Trading Post, the Crest Cafe, Anchor's Inn, the elementary school and Mahon Hall, the school auditorium.

We found three ferry terminals on the island: Vesuvius, located on the northwest side, sent smaller ferries to Crofton on Vancouver Island; Fulford, on the southern end, ran thirty-five minute ferries to Swartz Bay which was located on the Saanich Peninsula, north of Victoria; Long Harbour where larger ferries crossed the Strait of Georgia to the Tsawwassen terminal.

One night, while Maurie and I walked along a moonlit shore bordering Long Harbour, feeling dreamy, I said, "Wouldn't it be wonderful to have a cabin up here? This island is so beautiful."

"It *is* a beautiful island," Maurie agreed. "Maybe we could ride around with a realtor before we leave and see what property costs up here."

And so, before we left, we went with a realtor to see some properties for sale. We found one lot to our liking but the realtor wasn't sure if it was still for sale.

4

THE GREEN HOUSE

Two weeks after we returned from our holiday in Canada, a letter arrived from Cyril. I opened it and after reading it, I felt faint. I immediately called Maurie at the office.

"You don't sound so good, Jacque," Maurie said, "what's the matter?"

"Jack Russell is dead!" I was choked up. "We just got a letter from Cyril."

"Oh, my God! What happened?."

"Evidently Jack had a massive heart attack and fell out of bed. He was dead before he hit the floor. Maurie, how old was Jack?"

"Oh, I think he was only fifty-six or fifty-seven."

"Poor Migs. It's going to be tough on Janet and Jim...being teenagers and losing their dad."

"I better call Migs and see what I can do to help. What a shame."

Maurie called Migs in Canada and he said she sounded devastated. He went to work right away to help her with legal affairs in San Diego. Since Jack was an American citizen, a United States federal estate tax return had to be filed and his American properties probated. Maurie worked by letter and phone with Migs and her Canadian lawyer, Paul Beckmann. However, the wheels of probate ground slowly.

Finally, in February, Maurie said, "I want to fly to Vancouver to see Migs and Paul. I need more information. Why don't you come with me, Jacque?"

"I don't know. I have mixed feelings about going under such unhappy circumstances," I answered. "Besides, I'd have to ask Mom and Dad to baby-sit the kids."

"I think it will be helpful to Migs for us to be there. She needs our support. After seeing her in Vancouver, maybe we can take a ferry to the island and relax over the weekend."

"Could we see the Cunninghams and Salt Spring again?"

"Sure. Why don't I call the Cunninghams and see if we can stay with them?" Maurie said.

Cyril and Carrie Louise gladly invited us for the weekend. My parents were free to baby-sit, so I decided to go.

Such a sad reunion in Vancouver. Migs, Janet and
Jim were broken-hearted over the loss of Jack. Migs
braved her situation valiantly. I remember how we
talked with her over lunch. She told fascinating stories
about her married years with her entrepreneurial husband. Then she described how they discovered Long
Harbour.

"Jack first heard about Salt Spring from Charles
Moat during World War II," Migs said. "Jack went in
with MacArthur's forces in '45 to release and protect
prisoners in the Philippines. It was there Jack met
Charlie, who had been a prisoner and was interned by
the Japanese for four years. Charlie was a Canadian
from Vancouver and had come out to the islands on
business. By the way...Charles Moat was no relation to
the Mouats who own the store in Salt Spring."

Migs said that Charlie and Jack struck up a phenom-
enal friendship. Charlie told Jack what sustained him in
prison was remembering the beauty of an island called
Salt Spring and a particular harbour that was like paradise called Long Harbour. Charlie dreamed of buying
property on the island someday.

"Manila was heavily damaged," Migs said, "and
concrete blocks were needed for reconstruction. Jack
and his friend Jack Shafer saw the need, so after the war,
they started a concrete block factory in partnership;
Charlie joined the business later. Before the war I met
Jack at Cal Berkeley where he was studying mining
engineering. After the war, we were married and I went
with Jack to the Philippines."

"Didn't you go to Canada after the Philippines?" Maurie asked

"Yes," Migs answered, "the business was sold in the Philippines after great success and we all moved to Edmonton to start another concrete block factory. Charlie came out to Salt Spring in 1950 hoping to buy property on Long Harbour, but nothing was available. It was at that time he met an islander, Mary Lees, who became his wife. You know Mary Moat, don't you?"

"Yes," we replied.

Migs continued. "We visited Long Harbour out of curiosity and loved it just as much as Charlie. Then, in 1957, after we sold the Edmonton business, lots 9 and 10 on the northerly edge of Long Harbour came on the market. Charles and Mary bought lot 9 which had 160 acres with the old Lucky Baldwin house and dock and Charlie named the property Maracaibo. We bought lot 10 which had 250 acres out to Nose Point."

"Why did Charlie name it Maracaibo?" Maurie asked.

"I guess there's a beautiful hidden lake in Venezuela named Maracaibo that Charlie read about."

"So, when did you and Jack move to the island?" I asked.

"In 1967. We were living in Borrego Springs at the time when lot 8 was for sale. It was 160 acres on the other side of the Moats and it had a cottage. We bought the property and ended up spending our summers with the kids in the cottage. We called the cottage Toad Hall, you know, from the story, *Wind in the Willows*. When Jack wanted to sub-divide the property, we made our final migration up here in 1967."

"I know he was working on sub-dividing the peninsula," Maurie said.

Migs sighed. "He was so frustrated with the project. The government put a 10-acre freeze on all the Gulf Islands—meaning property could only be divided into 10-acre parcels and nothing less. I guess the government was trying to control development and sewage problems. Before Jack died, he made arrangements with Lansdale and Associates to join lots 8 and 10 with lot 9—since Charlie was not well and wanted to sell lot 9 to Lansdale—and the amalgamation was called the Maracaibo Association. But Jack didn't know at his death if he could build a road skirting Maracaibo that would go to Nose Point. There was no guarantee that water or power could be put in—at private expense. All the hassle probably brought on his heart attack. Did you know that Jack had one heart attack before? He was supposed to be careful."

"Yes, I did," Maurie replied, "he told me one time at my office."

"Now I don't know what's going to happen," Migs said.

"Give it time, Migs," Maurie suggested. "Perhaps Paul Beckmann and the Lansdale group will figure something out."

"Which reminds me." Migs looked at me. "I want you both to come to my apartment tomorrow night for dinner and meet Paul and his wife, Elizabeth."

The next night Migs proudly introduced us to the Beckmanns. Paul was tall, wavy-haired; his wife, Elizabeth, was a petite blond from Scotland. Paul looked the typical lawyer—conservative suit and tie, dark rimmed glasses. He was younger than Maurie and practiced with a large Vancouver firm. His easy smile and his outgoing manner made me like him immediately. Elizabeth's friendly blue eyes sparkled as she spoke. Because of the Beckmanns' amicable ways, what might have been a difficult gathering turned into a wonderful evening full of good feelings.

The following day I was anxious to board the ferry and head for Salt Spring. The ferry churned away from the Tsawwassen terminal and headed across the Strait of Georgia toward the Gulf Islands. Quiet settled into my heart. Relaxation overcame my body. Solitude settled in my soul. The heartache of Jack's loss faded away like the Tsawwassen skyline.

The Cunninghams were waiting for us at the Long Harbour terminal. Our reunion was happy indeed.

"We're sorry y'all came back under such sad circumstances, but we're so glad to see you again," Carrie Louise drawled.

There was non-stop chatter all weekend. The Cunninghams spoiled us with drinks by the fire followed by delicious dinners in their cozy dining room. Before our return to Vancouver, we drove them around the island in our rental car to show the property we had seen the previous summer. We took a loop around Scott Point to the south side of Long Harbour. I caught glimpse of a modern, green house tucked among the trees with a *For Sale* sign on the deck.

"Stop!" I shouted. "Back up, there's a green house for sale."

"A greenhouse?" Carrie Louise asked. "You mean where plants grow?"

"No, no," I said, "I meant a house that's green."

"Jacque, we don't have time to look at a house now," Maurie insisted, "our ferry leaves in forty-five minutes."

"It will just take a minute, pleeease?"

The four of us hopped out of the car and walked down the driveway. The yard leading to the house was brilliantly green with grass; soft spaghnum moss clung to the rocks; salal nestled beneath the trees. It looked like the Garden of Eden in the February rain. We found a modern split-level house overlooking the harbour. The *For Sale* sign had a realtor's phone number.

"Let's call the number from the Cunninghams, Maurie, and find out about the house."

Maurie sighed. "Here we go, getting involved."

The realtor said to me on the phone, "The key is hanging on a nail behind the railing by the first step and you're welcome to take a look around. You'll have time to see the house because it's only a mile from the ferry terminal."

In twenty minutes, the four of us took a hurried home tour. From the top deck we looked across the rippled waters of the harbour to Jack's verdant peninsula; a broken fragment of a small island lay snuggled next to a white, sandy cove.

Inside we discovered a cedar, prefab house. The upper level had a kitchen, dining area and living room from which beautiful views of the harbour were framed by cathedral windows. Two bedrooms and two baths were located on the back side of the house.

A stairwell in the middle led to the lower level. One large room with a view window and a brick pad for a wood stove was below; a small undeveloped room was adjacent. Both levels had decks with an outside stairway connecting them.

"Oh, Maurie, it's perfect," I said. "It's like a dream house. Wonder what they're asking for it?"

Half-heartedly Maurie answered, "Yeah, it's a nice house."

"It's a darlin' house," Carrie Louise said, her voice encouraging. "We'd love to have y'all up here on Long Harbour."

Cyril was enthusiastic. "I think you can get a good buy on this property. I'll be happy to take care of it for you."

Maurie looked at me. "I can tell by the look on your face that you really like this house. When the ferry reaches the mainland, I'll call the realtor and ask about the price. But the ferry leaves in a few minutes. Come on. We gotta hurry and catch it."

For two weeks Maurie negotiated long-distance by phone with the realtor about the price. I yearned for the house nestled in the woods overlooking Long Harbour. I visualized summers of boating, fishing, beachcombing, crabbing...far away from traffic and tourists.

Then, one night, Maurie said to me with a calculating look in his eye, "I figured out a way we can make a down payment on the house."

I threw my arms around him and squealed, "Maurie Watson, you're a financial genius! Let's do it. Mom and Dad said they would loan us a little money with interest, of course."

"Yes, and the owner agreed to carry the paper on the balance owing. So, my dear," Maurie said, "it may be a crazy thing to do, but we can buy it. However, we're going to have to sacrifice and be very careful with what we spend in the next few years."

Maurie phoned the realtor and arranged the purchase of the house. In March, 1973, when the closing of escrow was near, we packed our station wagon, rented a U-Haul trailer and filled it with used furniture. We headed north toward our dream house and toward a turning point in our lives.

5
SETTLING INTO
SALT SPRING ISLAND

The windshield wipers slapped furiously against the rain pelting down upon our station wagon. My heart felt as empty as the U-Haul trailer rattling behind. We lined up to board the ferry back to Tsawwassen. As we drove into the cavernous, near-vacant ferry hold, I began to wonder if it was smart to buy a house so far away. Don't have a faint heart, I told myself, wait 'til next summer when you return...things will look brighter.

The despair I felt in March gradually faded and I became excited about preparing for our return to Salt Spring the following summer in '73. The thrill of having a house on an island in another country spurred me on. My excitement grew as the days dwindled down for departure.

When we pulled into our driveway, after another 1,400 mile trip, the Garden of Eden we left in the March rains had disappeared. Tall, brown weeds sprouted over the septic tank, arbutus leaves dirtied the decks and cobwebs draped the doors.

"Yuk," the kids said, "this place looks awful."

That first summer was hot and dry, perfect weather for irascible wasps. "Every seven years, particularly when it's a dry summer, we get hordes of wasps." Carrie Louise informed us. Armies of carpenter ants marched over the carpets in full command. Sinks and showers were watering holes for giant, long-legged spiders.

Salt water leaked into the Scott Point community water well, so our tap water was brackish and undrinkable. "You'll have to go to Ganges to get water until Scott Point Water Works figures out what to do," Cyril told us. In the meantime, we ordered a water softener through the Simpson-Sears catalog and Maurie and Cyril installed it. At least we could bathe and wash clothes without that awful brown sediment.

It was a working vacation—moving furniture, cleaning every room and painting the two upstairs bathrooms. We hired a plumber to install a shower, sink and toilet in the small room on the lower level. The two levels began to look cozy—decorated with used furniture and mail-order curtains and bedspreads from Simpson-Sears.

There were endless trips to Mouat's to buy paint, hardware, tools, cleaning supplies and plumbing gadgets. The store was vital, not only to us, but to all islanders for it was the main source of building supplies. We slowly came to realize what an important part the Mouat family played in the island's history and development. The historical pictures hanging in Mouat's piqued our curiosity. They were pictures of the early family on the island dating back to 1885. Thomas William Mouat, a widower and a Scot from the Shetland Islands, migrated across the Atlantic Ocean and North America with his bride, Jane Manson Mouat, and seven year-old son, Thomas William; he came to live with his brother, Gavin Mouat, in Spokane, Washington.

Next, the family moved to Nanaimo on Vancouver Island to live with cousins, but the coal dust irritated Thomas Mouat's tuberculosis. The clear air of Salt Spring was recommended to him so he settled on the island and farmed the shore of St. Mary Lake where the family lived for twenty-two years.

Thirteen years after coming to Salt Spring, Thomas Mouat died of tuberculosis at age 45, after his eleventh child was born. Four children predeceased Jane Mouat, leaving four boys and three girls. The following years were a great challenge to Jane in raising a family and continuing with the farm. Jane's step-son, Thomas William, worked off-island in a Nanaimo mill and sent his earnings home to help support the family; William Manson Mouat, Jane's eldest son, had the burden of running the farm at age fourteen.

We were in Mouat's one day buying paint from Cyril when we met Ivan Mouat, William's son, who was the unofficial historian for the family.

I was curious about the store and asked him, "How did Mouat's get started?"

"Well, the story goes that my uncle Gilbert worked for Malcolm and Purvis, a general store on the island," Ivan answered. "Mr. Purvis called uncle Gilbert aside one day and said: 'Gilbert, our store is for sale and I want you to buy it. You've got a good business head.'

"'Thank you, Mr. Purvis,' replied uncle Gilbert, 'but I don't have any money.'

"'What happened to that $50 I paid you yesterday? That'll do,' said Mr. Purvis. An that's how Mouat's began. Grannie Mouat, that's what Jane Mouat was called, and Gilbert bought the store in 1907. They called it G.J. Mouat and Company. Grannie became the postmistress of Salt Spring in 1908 and had the post office in the store. In 1909, Dad's uncle Gavin lent him $2,000 so he could join the business and it was then called Mouat Brothers and Company."

We learned that the white building with the dark green trim was built in 1912 and was called Mouat Brothers and Company Limited. The old Malcolm and Purvis building, adjacent to the new Mouat's, became a boarding house known as Grannie's Boarding House because Jane Mouat ran it; in 1957, the building was torn down after being used for business rentals.

Ivan told us about working as a boy at Mouat's in the 1930's.

"Gilbert was manager and president of the company. William, my dad, looked after the accounts. I worked in the feed shed, delivered groceries and waited on customers after school, Saturdays, and on holidays as did my cousins. In those days Mouat's sold hardware, lumber and groceries. The store was the Imperial Oil agent and the Ford dealer too. We had a candling room to check the quality of the eggs brought in by the farmers. There wasn't a bank on the island until after World War II, so the store used to give 90-day credit and acted like a bank.

"I remember in the 1930s Mouat's would bury you on Salt Spring Island for $35. Alan Cartwright, a Mouat truck driver, used the store truck to pick up the deceased from the home or hospital, laid out the body in a coffin he made from clear cedar shiplap, then shined up the truck as a hearse to take the coffin to the grave site. It was a service that Mouat's provided at no profit. The clergyman, the gravediggers, and the organist divided up the money."

"Grannie Mouat and Gilbert started a real family operation," I said. "When did Grannie Mouat die?"

"In 1935." Ivan replied. "Oh, yes, then there was Uncle Gavin, Dad's younger brother, who was a mover and shaker on the island. After being a partner for about 20 years in Salt Spring Island Land Development, which dealt in real estate and insurance, he bought the company and later called it Salt Spring Lands. He gathered signatures and convinced the Nanaimo-Duncan Utilities Company to bring power to the island in 1936-37. Then he bought and developed the Salt Spring Island water district. He was the driving force behind the building of the Ganges Secondary School in 1940 and the new Lady Minto Hospital in 1958."

"He had a big influence on the island," I said.

"Indeed he did," Ivan replied. "Why, he extended the ferry service to the island by buying the Fulford-Swartz

Bay route owned by Coach Lines of Victoria. He called
it The Gulf Island Ferry Service and later added the
Vesuvius-Crofton run and the inter-island service. "
   "Was that the forerunner of the British Columbia
ferries?" I asked.
   "Yes, Premier W.A.C. Bennet and the Social Credit
government established the B.C. Ferries in 1960 and
built the *Queen of Sidney* and *Queen of Tsawwassen.*
Then they bought Uncle Gavin's company in 1961."
   Mouat's changed ownership in 1969, a few years
prior to our coming to the island. Mouat Brothers
Limited, owned by William, Gilbert's sons and other
family members, liquidated and sold the assets. Jessie
Mouat Toynbee, Jane's youngest child, had three sons,
Dick, Manson and Tom. Dick and Barbara Toynbee,
Manson, Norman Mouat and John Lees became the new
owners and formed Mouat's Trading Company; the
transaction included a vacant lot adjacent to the old Salt
Spring Trading Company.
   Mouat's Trading Company, under Dick Toynbee's
leadership, acquired reclaimed pieces of upland property in Ganges and applied for a government permit to fill
in the land between those pieces to create the core parking area. When the permit was granted in 1970 and the
fill completed, Mouat's Trading Company erected two
buildings: a two-story building, which housed Ben's
Lucky Dollar Grocery Store, later the K & R Grocery
Store, now called the Harbour Building and the post
office presently housing a children's store. In 1972 the
floor beneath Mouat's was revamped into a mall containing small shops; the metal sheds adjacent to the mall
were converted from warehouses to additional shops,

such the Pegasus Art Gallery and Volume II Bookstore in 1977.

Tom Toynbee became managing director of Mouat's Trading Company in 1975. I first met Tom in the 1973 through Migs and the Cunninghams; they were neighbours at the end of Long Harbour. He and his attractive wife Yvonne were managers of Maracaibo for four or five years. "I used to call the island 'The Rock' when I was growing up," he told me. "My family and I lived at the end of Churchill Road overlooking Ganges Harbour—a great spot to live."

After Tom took over Mouat's, he later confessed, "I found Mouat's had a real financial problem—not enough money coming in and too much going out. So I devised a plan to stabilize our financing. I sat down with Dick and said, 'Here's the plan, it doesn't allow us to get paid until our overdue bills are taken care of.' Dick backed off from the business part and worked as our truckdriver hauling our building materials from Vancouver and Victoria for resale four or five days a week. It was a struggle for us and the other owners."

It seemed wherever we went, the Mouat name popped up. The island's provincial park encompassing about 80 acres located at the bottom of Ganges Hill was named Mouat Provincial Park. Gavin Mouat contributed the land in his family's name in 1961. There seemed to be countless aunts and uncles and dozens of cousins. Mouat's two-story white store with its dark green trim and Canadian flag flying high was not only an historical landmark but also a reminder of an influential island family.

Migs stopped by, often. Sometimes she came across the harbour in her little boat or she drove around Long Harbour in her car. She dealt with the loss of Jack by immersing herself in making pottery for ArtCraft, the summer-long show held at Mahon Hall featuring arts, such as weaving, paintings, blown glass and woodworking. One day she tapped on our back door and called through the kitchen window, "Hello, anybody home?"

We opened the door and there Migs stood holding two bundles wrapped in newspaper.

"What a nice surprise to see you," I said, "please come in."

Migs stepped inside the kitchen and put the two bundles on the counter.

"What do you have there?" Maurie asked.

"I've been throwing pots," Migs said, "that's what we say in the pottery business. I made a couple of things I thought you might enjoy."

"How great," I said.

"Go ahead and open them," Migs insisted. "You must remember these are some of my first attempts at making pottery."

I opened the larger bundle first. It was a forest green, ovenproof covered casserole dish. "How beautiful," I said, "it's just what we need. This must have taken lots of work to make."

"Well, there's a certain process you have to go through to make it all fit, but I've enjoyed doing the pottery this summer. It's kept me occupied and it's something creative for me to do."

"Jacque," Maurie said, "you better try out that dish for dinner tonight."

"Yeah," I agreed. I was full of curiosity about the smaller bundle. "May I open the second one now?"

"By all means," Migs said.

The bundle contained a small vase. "How lovely. But it's so different."

Yes, it *is* different," Migs said. "I used the Japanese technique called Raku to fire it."

"What's Raku?" Maurie asked.

"The vase is fired at a very hot temperature in an outdoor kiln made of concrete blocks. The heat causes the colors to assimilate into the vase."

"It's beautiful. I like the textured look," I said. "Thank you so much for both things."

"I thought they would go well in your house." Migs' blue eyes sparkled with pleasure. "Consider them as housewarming gifts."

"Thank you, Migs. How about a cup of coffee?" Maurie asked.

"I've got some cookies from Embe Bakery," I added.

"That would be nice," Migs said. "Do you know that that bakery is a historical site?"

"Really? What's so special about it?" I asked.

"Originally it was a creamery, famous for Salt Spring butter. It was the mainstay of the farming community."

"It's our mainstay for bread and cookies." I answered.

"I've got good news about the Maracaibo Association, Maurie."

"What is it?" Maurie asked.

"The government has lifted the 10-acre freeze!" Migs' eyes danced with delight.

Maurie smiled at Migs. "Terrific. That's really good news."

"I am so relieved, Maurie." Migs laughed. "Do you know, just as an aside, that the Maracaibo Association was first called the 'Maracaibo Syndicate,' but everyone thought it sounded too much like the Mafia."

Maurie laughed, "Ah, the Maracaibo Mafia. Will they be able to subdivide now?"

"Eventually. A road out to Nose Point will have to be built first." Migs continued talking about Maracaibo over coffee. Her conversation was always lively and informative, revealing an intelligent woman who had not missed a beat. Suddenly, she looked at her watch. "I nearly forgot Daphne."

"Who's that?" I asked.

"My friend from Edmonton who's arriving on the 4:30 ferry at Fulford. I have to go and pick her up. Thanks very much for the coffee."

We both gave her a big hug. "We really appreciate your gifts," I said. Migs hurried out the door. Watching her drive away, I thought, *If it hadn't been for Migs and Jack, we would never have discovered the island... wouldn't Jack be pleased to know his dreams of privately developing Maracaibo are coming true.*

There was another visitor too—who announced herself with a loud knock at the back door. There stood a short, sober-faced woman with big, round eyes. In a firm voice, she said, "You're not to leave your garbage bags on the road on collection day. The crows will peck at them and make a mess of your garbage. Use trash cans!"

Who is this lady?

"And remember, only white toilet paper will work in your septic tank...that coloured, fancy stuff doesn't disintegrate. By the way, I'm your neighbour, Kas Black." And she left.

A week later, another knock on the door. The same woman, but this time with plastic bags full of vegetables from her garden and freshly baked bread. She seemed more friendly. "Here's some warm bread for you and I just picked these vegetables."

"How kind of you," I said.

"A word of warning. Be careful what you leave outside because the Beachcomber has sticky fingers, eh? He grabs anything he can get his hands on. He's an odd one. By the way," Kas asked, "would you like to come to supper at our place tomorrow night? You can bring the kids." Her invitation surprised us.

We looked at each other. "Sure," Maurie said, "We'd be delighted to come." Kas departed abruptly again.

The Blacks' modest mobile home was situated on a picturesque site near the mouth of the harbour. It was the only dwelling beyond our house on Marina Crescent

Drive. Archie Black greeted us at the door. "Glad to meet you folks. Welcome to Scott Point. Come on in."

Kas' dinner of crab bisque, fresh vegetables, home-made biscuits and blackberry pie stuffed our stomachs. The Blacks' hospitality made us feel at home.

"So, you're a lawyer, eh?" Archie asked Maurie.

"Yes," Maurie replied. "What kind of work do you do?"

"Well, I'm a retired pharmacist. But I work a couple of days at the Ganges Pharmacy to keep out of mischief." Then Archie asked, "Do either of you play golf?"

"No," Maurie said, "with the kids and my practice, we don't have time."

"Well, we play. If you're ever interested, we have a fine, nine-hole regulation course in the central part of the island. The only problem is that the fairways have brown grass," Archie laughed, "just the greens are green...not enough water."

"Maybe we'll have time someday to join you." Maurie said, then looked at his watch. "Jacque, it's time we took the kids home and put them to bed. Thanks for the wonderful dinner."

When we crawled into bed that night, I said to Maurie, "Archie is nice and beneath Kas' blunt veneer is a generous heart." I lay my head on the pillow ready for sweet dreams. It was a warm summer night so our bedroom window was open. Suddenly I heard faint footsteps around the back of the house next to our bedroom.

"Maurie," I whispered, "there's someone walking outside."

Leaves crunched.

"Yeah, I heard the noise. I'll get a flashlight and shine it through the screen."

We carefully parted the curtains and Maurie pointed the flashlight outside. Four brown eyes reflected the light...and four pointed hairy ears twitched. Two deer were casually munching maple leaves.

"Whew!" I said. "For a moment I thought it was the Beachcomber."

The deer continued to eat, undisturbed. Amused, we watched them for awhile. We learned that black-tailed deer, wild and multiplying, were thieves in their own way on the island. They relentlessly grazed in vegetable gardens and flower boxes, causing islanders to use expletives as they covered everything with chicken wire.

"I feel silly," I said, "being frightened by deer," and went promptly to sleep.

6
TROUBLES

Although the B.C. Ferry Corporation advertised as "The Friendship Fleet," the summer of 1973 was when the British Columbia ferries weren't so friendly.

The B.C. Ferry Corporation, subsidized by the provincial government, was one of the largest ferry systems in the world. The ferries connected passengers and vehicles to ports of call throughout the province, including the southern Gulf Islands. The ferry was the one reality that bonded us all together on the island. It was our crucial link to civilization.

During the weekdays, the Long Harbour ferry transported only a few lonely souls seated on the decks or inside, mostly islanders, to and from Vancouver. On the weekends, passengers on holiday increased ten-fold. They peered through the windows, filled the decks on sunny days, and gave a happy aura to the ship.

In the middle of the summer came rumors of a possible ferry strike. Scott's friend Steve and our niece Lynn had flown up to be with us on the island. Having four kids to entertain with picnics, fishing and berry picking, Maurie and I paid little attention to the C.B.C. (Canadian Broadcasting Company) coverage of contract negotiations. However, a special bulletin on the radio grabbed our attention:

> "Negotiations for a wage increase for B.C. ferry workers have failed. The provincial government has not met the union demands and a ferry strike is imminent. Commuters to the Gulf Islands are urged to remain on the mainland or on Vancouver Island. All shipments and mail will be discontinued. Vacationers are advised not to use the ferries because the length of the strike will be indefinite."

"We'll have to cut Steve and Lynn's stay short and get them home right away," Maurie said, "otherwise who knows when they'll get back to San Diego. I'll call Pacific Western Airlines and see if I can move the kids' flights up to tomorrow."

Good luck, Maurie, I thought. *Our experience with P.W.A. has not the best.*

Maurie phoned the airlines and hung up with a smile on his face. "The kids can fly out of Victoria tomorrow at 1 in the afternoon and then connect in Seattle with a United Airlines flight to San Diego at 3. So, we better catch the 6:30 A.M. ferry tomorrow out of Fulford Harbour to Swartz Bay and beat the crowds."

The next morning we sped along the Fulford-Ganges Road with four kids giggling in the back seat.

"Be quiet, you guys," Maurie barked. "I want to listen to the radio and hear what's happening to the ferry strike."

> "Attention, attention. The B.C. ferry employees will begin their strike at midnight tonight. Check ferry schedules for last sailings on your route. We repeat, there will be no more sailings after midnight tonight."

"Terrible news," Maurie said. "It's a good thing the kids are flying out today."

I gasped when we approached the Fulford Harbour terminal. Milk trucks, courier vans, dump trucks, R.V.s, cars, Salt Spring Freight trucks, buses, vans carrying canoes were backed up the road. Horns were blasting. Cyclists, bikers, foot passengers and hikers huddled in lines like refugees evacuating from the war zone.

"So much for beating the crowds," I said.

Maurie frowned at me. He walked down to the ticket booth and returned with a sour look on his face. "We have to wait for two ferry crossings," he said, "which means we'll arrive at Victoria Airport at 11:30. But we'll get there in time for the plane."

I felt a headache coming on.

Being cramped in a mini-submarine 3,000 leagues under the sea would have been easier than being confined in a station wagon with wriggling kids for three hours. When we finally boarded the small ferry, I thought it would sink with its heavy load of vehicles and passengers. We disgorged ourselves at Swartz Bay along with the mobs. A caravan of cars headed toward Victoria Airport and we followed in line.

The airport was worse than the ferry terminal. Luggage was piled high inside the terminal making an obstacle course to the Pacific Western desk. People clamored around the check-in counter. Finally, at 12:30, we handed the flight tickets to the P.W.A. agent for check-in, feeling great relief that we made it.

"The P.W.A. flight is running late from Calgary," the agent said.

"What do you mean?" My head throbbed. "We have two kids who have to catch a 3 o'clock plane in Seattle."

"Sorry. You'll have to wait until the plane arrives, then decide if they'll make the connection. Next person, please."

An half hour passed, then came the announcement over the loud speaker:

> "The Pacific Western Airlines flight #162 from Calgary to Victoria has been delayed for one hour. Those passengers with connecting flights are advised to check at the P.W.A. counter."

We scrambled back to the check-in desk. The agent told us, "If I put your children on the flight arriving from Calgary, then going onto Seattle, there won't be enough time for them to make their 3 o'clock connection. There are no other flights today. Here's a rain check. You must reschedule their flights for another day."

"But there's a ferry strike starting at midnight and we live on Salt Spring Island," Maurie angrily shouted at the agent. "How in the hell are we going to get them back here?"

"I know there's a ferry strike, but I'm sorry, there's nothing I can do about it." The agent shrugged his shoulders.

"There is ONE THING we can do, " I yelled above the noise.

"What's that?" Maurie shouted back.

"Catch the next ferry back to Fulford before the strike begins,"

"Let's go."

The six of us were like salmon swimming upstream—fighting airport traffic, queuing up at Swartz Bay for another two-ferry wait and struggling for a place on the ferry. We arrived home around 8:30, exhausted. It was a day of futility.

When the house was quiet and the kids were asleep, Maurie and I stepped outside on our deck in the dark of night. "Discouraging day, wasn't it?" he said as he folded me into his arms.

"We still have the same number of kids we started with this morning. Plus I have a full-blown headache."

"We'll figure something out to get Lynn and Steve home."

The ferry returned to her berth that night. Her ship's lights sparkling under the starry sky. Her spotlight beaming down the harbour in search of the red channel marker positioned in front of our house. Her passing signaled the close of the day and the beginning of the strike. The harbour stood quiet early the next morning.

Life came to a halt on the island. Building materials and hardware were in short supply. There were few tourists in the shops. Food stores had limited stock and many empty shelves. Our canned and frozen food disappeared quickly. We ate lots of rock cod and crab caught in front of our house. Desserts consisted of wild blackberries picked from vines. There was no mail. We felt cut off from the rest of the world. Islanders constantly talked about the strike. Each day we clung to the T.V. or the radio for strike reports.

A week later, Maurie arranged to take the kids by water taxi from Ganges Harbour to Swartz Bay, then catch a cab to the airport and put them on the plane. This time his plan worked. When he returned to the island, he heaved a sigh of relief. "The kids are on their way. Now, I hope the strike ends before we have to go home."

Two weeks passed. We were on vacation but we were on edge. A dark mood prevailed on the island. A touch of anxiety overshadowed our days.

Then, the strike was settled as suddenly as it had started. An air of relief swept over the island...and into our hearts. It was wonderful to see islanders wearing smiles and to know our link with civilization was reconnected. Our daily routine resumed, unencumbered by the threat of being cut off from the world. Ferry service began immediately as if nothing had happened and the ebb and flow of ferry traffic washed upon the island's shores once again. The island blossomed like a flower after a long drought. Streams of tourists flooded the shops. Goods and groceries overloaded shelves. The light-hearted feeling of summer crept quietly back into our souls.

Yet, there were complaints about the wage agreement. "The B.C. government is paying the ferry workers far too much money for what they do," Cyril told us.

"Those ferries have us just where they want us," griped Kas. "The fares will go up and up. But what can we do? We're captives."

When the mail resumed, a brief note arrived from Steve:

> "Salt Spring Island is a nice place to visit
> but because of the ferries, I wouldn't want
> to live there. Thank you for the nice time."
>   Steve

In a few years, a larger ferry was assigned to the Long Harbour berth, the *Queen of Nanaimo*. She travelled round-trip a couple of times a day from Long Harbour to Otter Bay on Pender Island, to Village Bay on Mayne Island, to Sturdies Bay on Galiano and to the Tsawwassen terminal on the mainland.

The ferry's 130 meter length made her seem as large as an ocean liner. She was capable of carrying 190 vehicles and 1,200 passengers. I was accustomed to seeing her hulk slip quietly by each morning with passengers crowded for breakfast in the ship's cafeteria located on the stern. I welcomed her ship's lights at night—her spotlight searching for the red marker in front of our house. She was like an old friend returning.

She was a colourful picture floating along the water-way; her white hull painted with a stylized B.C. flag of a yellow sun surrounded with rays of blue and red; her gunnels trimmed with stripes of blue and red; the dog-wood emblem decorated the blue funnel; the B.C. and the dogwood flags flew at midship; the Canadian flag with its bright red maple leaf fluttered on the stern. A coat-of-arms under the captain's bridge read *Splendor Sine Occasu,* meaning in Latin *With Undiminished Splendor;* the saying captured the essence of being aboard watching the natural beauty float by.

Whenever she departed the harbour, she gained speed. Her horn blasted in warning as if to say, "Watch out, here comes the queen."

Toward the end of the summer, when we were anti-cipating our return to San Diego, Maurie pulled me aside one day, "Jacque, let's take a walk."

I felt uneasy about his invitation. *Something's wrong.*

"Look," he said as we strolled toward the ferry land-ing, "I've been doing some figuring about the house. I didn't realize the non-resident insurance would be so expensive. When I add the cost of our mortgage payments and estimated property taxes, it's going to be difficult to carry the house. Building the downstairs bath cost more than I figured so we used up our reserves."

My heart sank. *And I insisted we build the downstairs bath.* "Well, what do you suggest we do?" I asked.

"I don't know. We can't carry the house for very long."

There was a heavy silence. *Maurie was lukewarm about buying up here in the first place. We can't lose the house. I've got to think of something.*

Then I had an idea.

"How about renting the house for nine or ten months to pay for the costs? I'll do anything to hang on to it. Let's spread the word around that we're renting the house. Even advertise in the island newspaper. Tomorrow I'll go to the school office and find out if some teachers need to rent during the school year."

"O.K. We have to do something...if we want to keep the house."

I discovered no teachers were interested in renting. I listed an ad in the *Gulf Islands Driftwood* newspaper. I asked the Cunninghams, Migs and the Blacks if they knew anyone wanting to rent. I began to feel desperate.

We thought it a stroke of good luck when Dr. Kensington-Smyth called at the house inquiring about possible rental. He was a white-haired, gentle-spoken Englishman neatly dressed in a coat and tie. He introduced himself and said, "I've just come to the island and have joined a medical clinic. I need to rent a place for my wife and four children."

We were so eager to rent the house that we didn't inquire further. We thought the distinguished-looking man would make an excellent tenant.

"We want to rent on a ten-month lease," Maurie said.

"That's agreeable with me."

"Then bring your family by and we'll sign the lease," Maurie told him.

On the afternoon before we were to leave the island, our spotless, furnished house awaited the Kensington-Smyths. I felt so happy we found a tenant...that is, until the doctor and his family arrived. Out of the car came the dignified doctor followed by a heavy, sloppy woman with stringy black hair and four unkempt, barefoot children.

"I'd like you to meet my family," he said.

I shuddered within. *I think we've made a mistake. His family looks like a bunch of ruffians. What can we do...our time is running out.*

"Come into the house and we'll sit at the dining room table while, doctor, you can review the terms of the lease," Maurie directed. Their children ran upstairs and downstairs tracking in dirt from outside; our children played quietly in the bedroom. I sat there sickened at the prospect of renting to this family but I couldn't bring myself to say anything.

After the doctor signed the lease, Maurie suggested, "Let's have a drink on it." *Maurie must feel jubilant...I feel terrible!* When we raised our glasses for a toast, the doctor stared at his glass. His hand shook noticeably and he quickly downed the drink in one gulp.

How strange. The way the doctor took that drink.

That last night I lay in bed terrified. I woke Maurie. "I'm really upset about renting to those people. By the looks of that wife and children, I don't think they'll take care of the house. Is there something we can do to protect ourselves?"

"They'll be O.K. He's a responsible doctor. If it will make you feel better, I'll phone the insurance agent tomorrow and increase our coverage before we cross the border. Now let's get some sleep. We have an early morning ferry to catch and a long day of driving." Maurie turned over and started snoring.

The next morning we stood on the deck of the ferry as it peacefully passed our house. The cathedral windows reflected the gold of the morning sun. All was quiet. All was serene. Seagulls swooped overhead as if to say goodbye. Our dream house stood quietly on the high bank; I gazed longingly at it until it disappeared from view. My heart felt a wrench as the ferry gained speed out of Long Harbour. "I hope everything will be all right this year," I said as I put my arms around Maurie's waist and held him tight.

"You worry too much," he said as he clung to me.

After three days of driving south in heat and traffic, we arrived in San Diego. Two days later, the telephone rang.

"Hello, Mrs. Watson?"

"Yes, this is Mrs. Watson," I answered.

"This is Mrs. Kensington-Smyth...something terrible has happened to your house."

Terror struck my heart. "What's happened?" I asked nervously, again seeing the last glimpse of our house from the ferry, as it stood serene and beautiful, less than a week before.

"Your house caught fire last night."

"Our house caught fire! Good God, how did that happen?" I asked in disbelief.

"Some burglars broke into your house while we were asleep," Mrs. Kensington-Smyth said. "They stole our camera, our money and some other things. Then they set the house on fire."

"How much damage was done?"

"Just the back door and the back deck were burned. And the couch and the wall behind it."

"Oh, no." My mouth was dry. My heart was pounding. I broke out in a cold sweat.

"Then somehow the stairwell caught on fire too...some of the stairs burned. The children discovered the fire in the night and put it out with the hose by the back door."

"Did you call the police...or the fire station?"

"Yes, we called the Mounties this morning and they came to inspect the house. Don't worry, Mrs. Watson, everything is under control. We can take care of the repairs and send you the bills."

"Mrs. Kensington-Smyth, I *am* worried. We're coming back to the island as soon as possible. In the meantime, we'll call Cyril Cunningham who manages the house and he'll come by to see the damage. Until we arrive, don't do a thing."

I hung up muttering to myself. *Oh dear God, what will Maurie say? First, we're short of money for the house and now this.* I started to cry. *It isn't fair. I knew those people couldn't be trusted.*

In three days we arranged for airline tickets to Canada and for Maurie's parents to care for the children. I felt anxious and disheartened as our plane landed at the Victoria Airport, a week to the day after we left. *I got us into all this trouble...wanting that stupid house!*

The Cunninghams met us at Victoria Airport, looking glum. "Oh, you poor dears. What a dreadful thing," Carrie Louise said. "I can't believe all this trouble happened in only a week. Migs doesn't know the news yet. She went down to Redding to be with family for the winter. "

"What the hell happened, Cyril?" Maurie asked.

"I'll tell you all about it on the ferry," Cyril said, hurrying us along. "We must make the last crossing."

The ferry engines droned in the dark night. Cyril, with a grave tone in his voice, said, "I haven't been able to get inside the house because the Kensingston-Smyths wouldn't let me in. I told them I managed the house for you but they told me to go away. The back door and the deck next to it are badly burned. They've thrown burnt cushions and debris outside the back door onto the ground. Looks pretty bad."

"It's strange that they didn't let you inside," I said. "I told the wife you would inspect the damage."

"Never mind," Cyril answered. "You spend the night with us. Tomorrow morning you better go straightaway to the Royal Canadian Mounted Policeman and ask him what he found before you go to the house. We'll lend you our extra car."

Early the next morning we were in the office of the R.C.M.P.

"It's very strange," the policeman said, "I was not called by the Kensington-Smyths until 10 in the morning after the fire. Ordinarily, people call my office immediately when there's a fire or robbery. When I inspected the premises, it looked like the fire occurred in the early morning...not in the night. It's also unusual for children to put out a fire and not the adults. I wonder if there really was a burglary, eh?"

"I wonder too," Maurie said. "I want you to request an inspector to come from Vancouver and determine if there was a burglary...and the cause of the fire."

The Mountie protested. "Mr. Watson, sir, I don't wish to trouble the Vancouver office over this small incident."

"Look, this is not a small incident!" Maurie shot back. "We've owned this house less than a year. I verbally increased our insurance coverage over the phone last week after we rented the house to the doctor. Then the house caught on fire. Now, the insurance people give me the feeling that I am suspect. We've got to prove that we are not in cahoots with the doctor."

The R.C.M.P. reluctantly phoned the Vancouver office—then told us an inspector would arrive on the noon ferry the next day. *I am so thankful Maurie is a lawyer and can argue his case.*

I shall never forget the return to our ravaged house. Charred boards crunched beneath our shoes as we stepped on the back deck. Dusty ashes—filtering through the air—coated the railing and everything we touched. Rubble of grey and black, of latex cushion, of vinyl lay heaped on the ground beneath the deck. The blackened back door greeted us as if in mourning. I felt sick to the core.

Maurie knocked on the back door...bits of singe fell off. The doctor opened the door, looking remorseful.

"Please come in, Mr. and Mrs. Watson," he said. We stepped over the threshold onto scarred kitchen flooring. Mrs. Kensington-Smyth immediately took control of the conversation, chattering away in her New York accent. The doctor noticeably withdrew while she rehashed the story that burglars broke into the house, then started the fire.

Instead of the sweet smell of cedar, an acrid odor of smoke lay heavy inside the house. The cathedral windows had a dull pallor. We walked over blackened, water-spotted carpeting. One end of the couch was burnt with crusty remnants of vinyl and latex clinging to the sides. The rich sheen of the cedar paneling behind the couch was scorched.

"Somehow the stairwell caught on fire too," Mrs. Kensington-Smyth continued. We looked down the stairwell and saw soggy, singed carpeting curling up from burned stairs.

"It's a wonder this house didn't burn to the ground." I felt drained as I spoke.

The doctor, with an air of dignity, said, "The children saved the house by putting out the fire with your hose."

"Where are your children?" I asked.

"They're playing after school. We're to pick them up later," the doctor answered.

"And where were you and Mrs. Kensington-Smyth when all this happened?" Maurie asked.

Avoiding Maurie's stare, the doctor replied, "Why, we were in bed fast asleep."

"Well, at my request, an inspector from Vancouver is coming over to investigate all this," Maurie said. "He'll be here on the noon ferry tomorrow." The doctor blanched. An uneasy silence settled over the room.

"There's no need to do that, Mr. Watson," the doctor said, "we'll simply take care of the repairs and keep in close contact with you in San Diego."

"Sorry, the inspector will be here tomorrow," Maurie replied. We left the house without another word.

We decided to walk over to see the Blacks. Kas met us at the door and said, "Oh, am I glad you're up here. That's terrible about your fire. Come in. You better sit down. I've heard some things you'll want to know."

"Oh, Kas, this whole thing is such a mess." I sighed, "What have you heard?"

"Well, a friend of mine, who is a nurse at the Lady Minto Hospital, saw the doctor doing rounds the morning after the fire. She said his black pin-striped suit had soot stains and reeked of smoke She said he looked terrible." Kas raised her eyebrows and lowered her voice, "She claims he's writing prescriptions without a license."

I felt limp in my chair. *This is like being in a frightening dream from which I can't awaken.*

7

UP FROM ASHES

The inspector cautiously shook our hands with a questioning look in his eyes. I sensed he was suspicious of us. "I want you and the tenants off the premises for an hour and an half while I look things over," he said. "Then come back and get me."

Not knowing what to do with ourselves, we drove to Burgoyne Bay on the west side of the island. We walked out to a sheer cliff and looked at the stunning view in silence. The Sansum Narrows were like a silver-blue serpentine slicing the   shoreline of Vancouver Island from Salt Spring.   Below us in the bay were log booms—clusters of logs floating in the water ready to be towed to lumber mills. From our cliffside perch, the logs looked like matchsticks. A little tug boat struggled to push the many logs in place; it worked hard dipping and turning to round up the logs. I was struggling, like the little tug boat, with what to do about our situation.

I broke the silence. "I am so sorry I got us into this terrible mess."

Maurie angrily muttered, "First, there was the ferry strike, next we ran out of money for the house." His voice became louder. "Then we rented the house to cover expenses, the house catches on fire and nearly burns down. The Beachcomber was right...we really got STUCK on this island."

"For the first time, I'm beginning to feel that way too. Maybe the inspector will find some clues....or something. Maybe it won't be as bad as we think."

"You do realize that the cost of repairing everything will be expensive. I just hope there'll be enough insurance money to cover everything."

I stared blankly at the beautiful view. "I hope so too."

When we returned to the house, the inspector was standing in the driveway waiting for us. I dreaded hearing what he had to say.

"There was no burglary," he said. "There was no break-in. Your tenants are at fault. Someone left a smoldering cigarette on the couch and it caught a cushion on fire. I've seen this kind of thing happen many times. I suspect the doctor and his wife were drunk and went to bed. The cushion smoldered all night. The children discovered the cushion on fire in the early morning.

They carried it across the room and burning pieces, falling off, set the stairwell on fire. They threw it out the back door onto the deck and the door caught fire. Then they put the fire out with a hose."

Conflicting emotions hit me. I felt relieved we were no longer suspect. Then dread welled up within me. *Now we know what really happened...but how are we going to deal with these people?*

"I'll write up my report and send a copy to the insurance people...and I'll be happy to testify in your behalf as an expert witness in court, if necessary." The inspector smiled and gave us a strong handshake.

"Thank you for coming. Your inspection and report will help us a lot," Maurie said.

"Glad to do it. Now, will you take me to the ferry terminal?"

We drove slowly back to the house, discussing what we should do next. "We've got to get those people out of the house," Maurie said, "but I don't think it's going to be easy." We parked our car in the driveway and waited for them.

When the Kensington-Smyths arrived with their children, the wife was driving. The doctor was unsteady as he got out of the car, smoking a cigarette. The children ran noisily into the house.

We slowly approached the Kensington-Smyths. "Your burglary alibi won't work," Maurie firmly said to them. "The inspector told us what happened." Maurie recounted the inspector's step-by-step scenario. The doctor looked as if he anticipated what Maurie would say.

"All this time you two were in bed. The inspector suspects you were probably drunk," Maurie said. "It's your negligence that caused the fire. You've done considerable damage to the house. We want you off these premises as soon as you can pack your things."

The doctor whom we trusted had changed. His distinguished facade seemed to crack before us. He looked helpless and didn't speak. He stared sadly at us. I realized, then, he had been drinking.

His wife stepped in front of him like a New York "tough" and put her hands on her hips in defiance.

"We're not moving and you can't make us." She sneered at us. "Remember, we have a ten-month lease."

"After what you've done to our house, we have grounds to remove you," Maurie snapped. "If you don't cooperate and leave, we'll file a suit in Victoria and have you evicted."

"Mr. Watson, I told you...we're not moving! We'll fight you every inch of the way." The wife's eyes narrowed.

I felt sick to my stomach. I was scared. *We're getting deeper and deeper into trouble. That woman acts like she's a member of the Mafia.*

Maurie called Paul Beckmann for his recommendation for a good lawyer in Victoria. In September the lawyer started proceedings. There were delays. We received no rent money. No repairs were made on the house. Three months passed while we were in San Diego and the problem remained, hanging over our heads like a dark cloud.

Then, in December, Kas Black called. "Wanted to let you know the latest news on your tenants next door."

"What now, Kas?" I asked her, not really wanting to hear.

"The doctor was dismissed from the clinic because he's an alcoholic."

"I'm not surprised," I answered.

"And the Kensington-Smyths have accumulated lots of unpaid bills in Ganges, so the merchants don't like them. You should see the burnt pots, left-over food and trash they've deliberately thrown on the deck—it's disgusting."

When I repeated the news to Maurie, he became agitated. "What do you think about driving up there after Christmas?" he said. "I want to see the house and get that lawyer moving."

"Fine with me. We'll be tired after Christmas but we can do it. Well have to take the kids. I know the Cunninghams won't mind if we stay with them again."

It was a sickening sight—the assemblage of rotten food, destroyed pans, old newspapers and soiled paper sacks heaped upon the dark destruction from the fire. The carport was jammed with junk.

"Watch out when you knock on the door," I said to Maurie, "she's one mean lady."

"Here's one mean lady who has met her match." Maurie angrily pounded the back door.

Mrs. Kensington-Smyth opened the door, looked shocked to see us, tried to close the door, but Maurie kept it open with his foot.

"We've come to inspect the premises," Maurie said.

"I'm sorry, Mr. Watson, but you have to make an appointment to see the house." She glared at him.

"Then I'm making an appointment for five minutes from now." Maurie removed his foot and she slammed the door shut.

We waited in the driveway. "Prepare yourself for the worst," Maurie said to me.

When five minutes was up, Maurie knocked again. The doctor opened the door—he was drunk, a disgrace. His drunkenness made him assertive, so he pushed his wife aside when she tried to shut the door. "Let these people in, my dear. Please enter, Mr. and Mrs. Watson," he said with a flourish.

Symphonic music floated above the surreal mess. "Do you like classical music?" the doctor asked as if he were trying to blot out the whole situation.

Maurie ignored his question. "We're here to look the house over and to let you people know that we'll see our lawyer in Victoria tomorrow about your eviction. We're going to fight you until we get you're outta here."

"The wheels of justice grind slowly," the wife smiled defiantly. She followed us around the house like a hound dog. *I have a hunch she's dealt with the law before.*

The next day Victoria was cold and unfriendly. Winter winds curled around every corner. The warm, sparkling city of summer had changed its character as if it didn't want us there.

Over lunch, the lawyer said, "Eviction proceedings take time. I'm doing everything I can to make things happen. You'll have to be patient. At this point I can't tell you when the eviction will happen."

Discouraged and depressed, we returned to San Diego, believing our trip was to no avail.

In early February, we received notification that a court order was sent to the Kensington-Smyths to vacate the property. At the same time, the Canadian Immigration Department named them "undesirable" and made arrangements to deport them back to England.

Into the void left by bad people, came some good people. My parents offered to help us with the house. My father, Bud Whiteman, retired chief of Orange County Police Communications, possessed an innate mechanical ability—he could fix anything. My mother, Helen, never retired from housekeeping—she was a creative soul. They made a good rescue team. If it hadn't been for them, we might have lost the house.

They arrived on the island just in time to oversee the tenants' departure.

"Your tenants got out of here yesterday." Dad said on the phone.

"I wish I could have been there," I replied.

"You should have heard the R.C.M.P. when he packed those people up and moved them out. He told them, 'If either of you step foot on this island again, I'll arrest you.'"

Mother got on the phone, "A really strange thing happened last night. We took the Cunninghams to dinner at the Harbour House Hotel. Who should be in the dining room but your former tenants eating and drinking to the hilt. The Canadian government put them up at the hotel before shipping them off to England. The children were noisy and the doctor and his wife were both drunk."

Then she sounded hesitant, filling the phone line with a lot of chatter as if she were avoiding the real news.

"Mom, you're not telling me everything. What's the matter?" I asked.

"Well, I hate to say this, but your place is in really bad shape."

My stomach twisted. "What did they do?"

"They clogged the toilets with glue...on purpose. Light switches and plugs are dangling from their sockets..." Mother paused again.

"Go on, tell me everything. I can take it," my brave voice belied my suffering within. Guilt consumed me. Here my parents were cleaning up a nasty mess left by sick, deranged people—all because I wanted a dreamhouse in Canada.

"They left burnt ice trays on the stove. Crayon marks, scratches and holes are all over the cedar walls. It was deliberate destruction. Splintered drawers and cracked shelves are strewn in each bedroom. It's just as well you're not up here."

"What vengeful people," I said with sadness. "Mom, I just feel terrible putting you through all this. I feel like I'm a little girl again and have badly scraped my knees like I used to. And you and Dad are there to pick me up and put bandages on the hurts. Only the house is a real big hurt."

My parents stayed the month of February, which can be one of the worst months in British Columbia with cold winds, rain...and sometimes snow. Hardware, doors and lumber came by ferry—some days rough crossings brought delays to delivery.

Dad called us several times each week to tell us the progress. "Thank goodness Cyril works at Mouat's. He's found just the hardware and things I've needed. I don't know what I'd do without that store. I hired a carpenter and he and I just re-built the back deck. There's a new back door arriving on the ferry from Victoria. I just hope it fits into the new door frame we built."

"Thanks, Dad." I said. "My fingers are crossed...that the insurance money will cover our expenses."

"You should have seen the carloads of junk I've taken to the dump," Dad said. "Those people left your carport full of trash. By the way, all the light switches and plugs are operating now. Your mother and I are still working on the cedar paneling...sanding it and filling the holes. Cyril's been a big help. He's lent me his tools. He stops by almost every day to see how we're doin'."

My mother told me how she scrubbed, scoured, mopped, dusted and vacuumed.

"Honey," she said, "I washed the drapes and curtains at the village laundromat and now they're rid of that smokey smell. But what about the carpeting? Valcourt's is replacing it but they have a limited selection."

"Mother, it's up to you," I said. "Try to get nylon so it will be easy to clean and a color that will come as close to the old color."

"I'll try. By the way, we're going to the Cunninghams for a drink and dinner tonight. They've been so helpful. We've really gotten to be good friends."

"I'm glad. All of you have been such a wonderful help. I don't know what we'd do without you."

"And Kas Black has been over with pies and freshly baked bread. You know how your dad loves pies."

It was fortunate that the insurance covered all of the damages to the house. As the bills came into San Diego, our allotment for household replacement dwindled to $50.

"Everything is repaired or replaced...except the couch," Mother phoned. "You can take care of that next summer. We're going to leave in a couple of days."

"I can't believe you have been there a whole month," I said.

"Guess what?" Mother said. "Cyril has found a couple who want to rent the house until next July."

My heart felt a crunch. *We've just finished getting the house back in shape. Gee, I don't want any more problems with tenants.* "Mother, Cyril must ask for references. I want to be very careful and try to get reliable people. Have you met them? "

"Yes, they've been by the house. The husband is a chartered accountant who commutes to Victoria everyday. They have the money for the first and last months' rent plus a cleaning/damage deposit. He and his wife have some furniture so they don't care about not having a couch."

"We need the money, that's for sure...but no lease this time," I said.

Thank God the accountant and his wife worked out well.   When we arrived the following summer, the house looked cared-for and welcoming. Then, in the window of a Goodwill store in Victoria, we spotted a brown, reupholstered couch...with a $50 price tag. The exact amount left in the insurance fund.

We stood in our living room and looked at the brown couch in its new home. It looked good there. I thought about the Greek fable, the Phoenix, the mythological bird which burned itself to ashes and rose again to live a renewed life. Our house had survived its island pyre, the fire, the legal maelstrom. It took on a new life, inviting us to share the days that lay ahead.

8

ISLAND LIVING

A fresh look pervaded the house; it sparkled—the new carpeting, the new couch, the newly lacquered back door, and the clean draperies gave a crispness, an orderliness to the whole setting. A refreshed feeling welled in my heart knowing that the house was ours again, rid of the ugliness of the fire. Maurie seemed more enthusiastic. He surprised me when he suggested, "If we built a kitchenette on the lower level this summer, then with the downstairs bath, we would have a complete suite."

"For what purpose?" I asked.

"We could just rent the upstairs and have the down-stairs for our use only. If we got satisfactory tenants like the chartered accountant and his wife, we wouldn't have to move them out in a year. They could stay on and we could be downstairs during our vacation."

"And where are we going to get the money for this little project?"

"Well, the rent collected from the accountant has pretty much covered our mortgage payments and the Canadian property taxes. We still have to pay the insur-ance. And we'd have to pay for the kitchenette out of pocket. But I figure next year's rent should cover the costs of the kitchenette and everything else. In the long-run, I think having a downstairs suite would be a smart investment."

"Sounds good to me. I wonder if Simpson-Sears has one of those three-in-one stoves in their catalog. You know, the kind that has a stove and sink on top and a refrigerator below?"

"Yeah, good idea. I'll start asking around for a workman to do the job."

"Cyril told me workman on the island are in demand so you better start looking right away."

Maurie was unsuccessful finding a tradesman on island to do the job, but dear Cyril found someone from off-island who promised to come soon. And so, the building of the downstairs suite was launched, we thought.

◆◆◆

Since we didn't own a washer and dryer in those early years, I washed our clothes and linens at a broken-down laundromat located on a side road on the edge of Ganges. Mamas with babies, hikers with muddy clothes and hippies drying out from the rains popped their quarters into rumbling machines. Sometimes, the sweet smell of soap was overpowered by the sour smell of body sweat. When the odor in the cramped little room became too strong, I put my clothes in the washer or the dryer, left on an errand and inhaled fresh air.

That summer Maurie's parents visited us and I took May to the laundromat. We carried in our bundles of undies for two families to be washed along with the linens. An older couple and a young woman were busily loading the machines and folding dried clothes. May and I loaded several washers with our dirty laundry. The room smelled pretty good that day. The people looked neat and clean—and they were friendly. We stuffed the wet clothes in the dryers and decided to take a stroll to the nearby shops.

When we returned, the older couple met us at the door. "Was that young woman a friend of yours?"

"No," I replied, "why?"

"Well, she folded your laundry, put it in her car and left. People steal laundry around here, you know."

I looked at May in disbelief. "That's wonderful. Now we don't have any underwear." Panic set in. *I don't want to be with my in-laws without undies.*

"We think she might have driven into Ganges," the two said.

"What kind of car did she have?" I asked.

"It was that dark blue sedan parked right in front of the laundromat, remember?"

"Yes, I do. Come on, May, let's drive into Ganges and see if we can find her."

We cruised around the village which took two minutes. Then I spotted her sedan parked in front the R.&K. grocery store. I looked through the car window and it was piled with our checkered shorts, limp t-shirts and tired towels. I rushed into the store and ran breathlessly up and down the aisles looking for her. There she was, peering into the freezer section.

I stopped and composed myself. *Don't accuse her or start a fuss. Remain cool.*

I sauntered up to her. "Pardon me, ma'm, but I think you took the wrong laundry by mistake back there at the laundromat."

She looked up and was visibly shocked to see me. "What do you mean?" she asked.

"Well, I saw our linens and underwear in the back seat of your car. Perhaps you got confused. If your car is open, I'll just pick up those things that belong to us and be on my way."

She seemed relieved. "Go ahead. Take whatever you want."

Never again did I leave laundry unattended.

Saturdays included a trip to the Ganges Farmers' Market held in Centennial Park along the harbourfront; it was a local tradition not to be missed. Farmers, islanders and fishermen gathered to sell produce, flowers, baked goods, handknit sweaters, jams and seafood to make some extra money. Vans and trucks, wheelbarrows and card tables bordered the park promenade. Shoppers could choose from a mélange of fruits and vegetables—mounds of zucchini, freshly-pulled beets, orange carrots, delicate butter lettuce, snappy green and purple beans, succulent plums, strawberries and blueberries, island apples and blackberries carefully picked from wild berry patches.

Clusters of cut-off milk cartons containing huge, vibrant dahlias, dainty daisies, multi-colored mums, pastel snapdragons created an instant garden down the center of the promenade. Ladies sat proudly by their home-grown flowers and sold bouquets with a loving hand for very little money. British Columbia salmon, prawns, and Dungeness crab were available at the end of the promenade, all iced in the back of pick-up trucks, ready for sale.

The yeasty smell of baked goods, still warm from islanders' ovens, attacked my salivary glands on Saturdays; pies, cakes, cinnamon rolls, cookies, and dinner rolls, oh, so delectable! But my favorite of all the pastries was the sausage roll. What is a sausage roll? A rich, flaky roll, four to five inches in length, an inch across, wrapped around spicy pork sausage; an English tradition adopted by the Canadians. Such a versatile pastry—it could be eaten hot or cold for breakfast, lunch, dinner or when having tea.

The queen of sausage rolls appeared every Saturday morning peddling the tasty morsels from the back of her van. Stout yet regal, her crown a straw hat, she hawked her goodies until they sold out. Then she packed up her van and went home. The sausage roll queen was as much of a tradition as Farmers' Market.

Such bargain prices gave the local merchants keen competition. However, the market, being a weekly meeting place and a social gathering for news and gossip, encouraged islanders to linger in Ganges to shop, to go to lunch or to have a cup of coffee thus profiting village business. People wandered up Lower Ganges Road to Mahon Hall to visit ArtCraft.

In the following years, other vendors from off-island—booksellers, jewelry designers, potters, sellers of incense—began to infiltrate Farmers' Market. A variety of arts and wares mixed with the homegrown produce and the baked goods. It was the beginning of a commercial enterprise that no one could foresee.

Tortillas and *frijoles?* Few were available on the island then. Mexican food? A rarity—there were certainly no Mexican restaurants. And *tequila?* Islanders didn't know its other name was "ta-kill-ya." That's how it was on Salt Spring Island in 1974.

Since Mexican food was scarce, we decided to have a Mexican party that summer to thank the Cunninghams, the Blacks, the Beckmanns, and other islanders for their help with the house; we wanted to welcome Migs back from Redding.

We prepared for our first party before we left San Diego. Our station wagon was loaded not only with vacation gear, but also with *tortillas*, tins of beans and jalapenos, chips, and bright paper flowers from Tijuana. After we arrived and settled into the house, we excitedly called our neighbours and friends to come to our *fiesta*. We told them, "Our party is a way of saying *gracias, salud* and *olé* for your help this last year."

The day before the party our Salt Spring kitchen was transformed into a Mexican *cocina*. Carrie Louise helped me cook. We worked at the kitchen counter cleaning chilies, chopping garlic, shredding cheese, passing the time telling stories and laughing; while peeling the onions, we cried. Delicious aromas filled the kitchen as the *carne* cooked. We paused for a cup of Canadian tea and put up our feet. It was a good chance to visit and to be together in the warmth of the kitchen.

Tortillas were transformed into *burritos, tacos* and a chicken *tortilla* dish, or *enchiladas*. Canned refried beans, embellished with chopped garlic, minced onions and a dash of milk, tasted as if straight from Mexico. Tomatoes, chilies, onions, herbs, blended to a piquancy, became the *salsa*. An avocado mixture of chopped tomato, onion, chilies, lemon juice, seasonings and sour cream made *guacamole* and it was served as a dip for crisp *tortilla* chips. A green and gold salad, consisting of avocados, oranges, purple onions and romaine lettuce tossed with Italian dressing added a green garnish. A basket of warm *tortillas* completed the main course. Swirled Kahlua and ice cream, poured into small paper cups, offered a cool taste following the fiery food—a final touch to the *comida*.

Overnight, our rustic house became a *cantina* and a *casa para una fiesta*. We draped *serapes* with shocking colours on the serving tables. The Tijuana flowers and farmers' market dahlias graced the tables. Paper *servilletas* and plates with designs of *sombreros* added to the Mexican ambiance. To welcome guests, Mexican flags and a large floppy *sombrero* with embroidered letters *Acapulco* were posted at the front entrance.

Many dressed for the occasion, Latin style. Out of the wilds of the somber British Columbia forest ventured Canadians wearing colourful *rebozos* and *guayvera* shirts. Carrie Louise wore a full-length pink cotton Mexican dress embroidered with sprays of flowers; a delicately-fringed *mantilla* hung softly around her shoulders. Getting in the Mexican mood, Migs donned a short white embroidered dress cinched in the middle with a colourful, hand-woven belt.

Maurie deftly made sumptuous *margaritas* with lemon juice, *tequila*, triple sec, chopped ice and salt around the rim of the glasses. The light lemon-flavoured drink slips down the throat innocently. But beware *amigos*: The juice of the *agave* cactus, when too much consumed, can attack the *cabeza* and the stomach *muy pronto*. Islanders lapped up the *margaritas* with relish. After dinner we found an agave-stricken victim who got as far as our bedroom and fell like a cedar tree across the bed.

Later, a guest sidled up to me and asked in a whisper, "Have you seen my husband?" I can't imagine where he might be. I've looked everywhere—upstairs, downstairs, outside."

"Let's check the rooms again. Come on," I said.

We carefully peeked into each room without finding him.

"There's only one room where we haven't looked."

"Where?" asked the wife.

"In the small upstairs bathroom. There's a light shining beneath the door. It seems quiet in there. Shall we take a chance and look?" I suggested.

We knocked and there was no answer. Carefully, we opened the door. Behold, there was the husband sitting on the toilet, leaning against the wall, passed out cold with his pants draped around his ankles. His wife turned crimson at the sight. She quickly and and quietly pulled him together and led him out the back door without notice.

This was the first of many stories inspired by our *Fiesta Canadiana* that started as a thank you in 1974, but continued as a tradition over the years.

"Yes, Mr. Watson, I'll be there on Wednesday to install the cabinets downstairs." So said the tradesman, but we could never be sure. Sometimes he showed up a week from Wednesday. Our scowls when he finally arrived didn't faze him. In fact, after he installed the cabinets, it was the unwritten island etiquette to invite the workman in for a cup of coffee and a chat.

Simpson-Sears delivered the three-in-one stove a few days before our departure for San Diego. The pressure was on to finish the project. Maurie called and called the off-island workman, finally connected with him and begged him to drop everything and come to the island. In our hearts we sadly anticipated finishing the downstairs the following summer.

We were flabbergasted when the tradesman showed up the next day with tools in hand and a helper. They swiftly installed the plumbing and electrical for the stove unit, then built a wrap-around counter on the corner wall of the kitchenette. During the expected coffee and chat after the work was finished, the tradesman smiled and said, "You better paint that kitchenette before you leave."

That's impossible. I said to myself. *I have one day to pack, clean the house and defrost the refrigerator.*

However, at 5:00 A.M. the next morning, 24 hours before we were to leave, half asleep, we pried open the paint cans. Maurie said as he slapped paint, "I forgot to tell you about our new tenant."

"Yeah," I answered, carefully guiding the paint roller down the wall.

"He's a grocer and he comes from Sidney with excellent references."

"I'm glad." I could hardly keep my eyes open.

"He and his wife are building a home on St. Mary Lake. Their names are Dennis and Carol Scott. He wants to move in tomorrow after we catch the 6:40 A.M. ferry. Their linens are in storage so I promised him that our towels and sheets would all be clean for them. You'll have to go into the laundromat today."

Oh, no, not back to that smelly laundromat!

9

ISLAND CAR, ETC.

D riving south again at the end of that summer of '74, the towns between Seattle and San Diego became like a road map etched in my mind. The three-day tedium of sitting until muscles stiffened, being bored with scenery played in reverse and suffering the re-entry into L.A. smog, made me think, *Flying to Canada would be so much easier.* Then, I was thunder-struck with an idea.

"WHEELS! That's what we need on the island," I said.

"What do you mean, wheels?" Maurie looked puzzled.

"Instead of driving 1,400 miles from San Diego to Salt Spring and back every summer with two feuding kids in the backseat, we could fly up and back...if we had WHEELS...a car on the island!"

Maurie winced. "You know we can't afford that. We just finished building the kitchenette—there's no more money! Where are we going to get the money to buy a car?"

"I don't know," I sighed. Then I thought a moment. *Dad's such a car buff. Maybe he could find something cheap for us.*

"You're impossible," Maurie said. "First, you want a house on an island in Canada...that's hundreds of miles away, then..."

I interrupted him. "I bet Dad can dig something up this year. You know how crazy he is about cars. Maybe he can find an abandoned car through the police, or something."

"Your poor father. He takes a month putting our island house back together again and now you want him to find a car."

"I'll call him when we get home. It will be a wonderful project for him."

Sure enough, in the spring, Dad called. "I found a car."

"You have?" My heart leaped with joy. "I knew you would, Dad. Tell me about it." I said.

"Well, the price is right. It costs fifty bucks."

"Fifty bucks. You gotta be kidding."

"No, I'm not. It's got a few dents. A taxi hit it, but the motor runs fine. It's a '65 two-door Chevy Belair."

"Well, we can certainly afford that. Where did you find it?"

"Through a mechanic-friend. He wants to get rid of it."

"That's terrific. I can hardly wait to see it."

"Tell you what," Dad said, his voice excited, "if you and Maurie will cover the registration and insurance costs, we'll buy the car for you. Then your mother and I will drive it up to the island this spring and leave it there. Would your tenants mind if we stayed in the downstairs suite for a few days? We kinda like it up there."

I was ecstatic. "Dad, you're wonderful. Of course you can stay up there. We'll call the Scotts right away. I can hardly wait to tell Maurie."

In early July of 1975, Maurie drove us up to the island: the kids, Lynn and me with the boat coming along behind. He planned to fly home in a couple days because it was a busy time in his office with his law partner on vacation—then return in August.

Our aqua-blue island car awaited us in the carport upon our arrival. The fins on the rear fenders stuck well beyond the carport; the right one looked like crumpled foil. *Maybe that's where the taxi hit it.* The front grill had a curious curve like irregular teeth in need of ortho-dontia. There were four good tires but only three hub caps. A small, downward crack, appearing like an art deco design, was on the passenger side of the wind-shield.

The aqua-blue interior wonderfully matched the faded overhead ripped lining and exposed puffs of stuff-ing. Green upholstered seats, which Dad had cheaply covered, gave a sense of newness inside. Silver ducting tape covered cracks in the decaying dashboard. The steering wheel was a thin ring of aqua-blue plastic. Under the hood the rusty engine looked small inside the cavernous frame, unlike today's car engines that fill every inch between the front wheels.

Maurie stepped back, peered at our acquisition and said, "We have a two-tone car—blue and autumn rust." He shook his head. "I wonder how the taxi looks."

It was like working out in a gym to open and shut the two heavy doors groaning on their hinges. Inside, a distinctive musty odor filled the nostrils. Limp seat belts draped over the lap. Typical of Chevys built in the 60s, the motor idled with a roar and gunned with a mighty force.

Off we went, the car creaking and rumbling through the forest like a great blue tank. Occasionally the trunk popped open, obscuring the rear view, so we stopped the car and Scott jumped out to slam it shut. He later confessed how embarrassed he felt having to do that along the road. A consistent squeak drifted from the beneath the hood, sounding as if a bird nested there, but nothing ever flew out.

The Chevy was christened with the name, Island Car. We kept the weathered California black and gold license plates, adding registration stickers each year. An array of bumper stickers covered dents and rust spots, such as; *Beyond repair, We're spending our children's inheritance, No tubby roosters, Don't laugh, it's paid for, California girl.*

It was great fun to pile our house guests into Island Car, for it seated six, take the Fulford ferry to Swartz Bay and drive into Victoria. Tourists looked askance when we drove our beleaguered heap to the entrance of the Empress Hotel, asked for valet parking and emerged in all our finery for high tea.

There were new neighbours that summer. We were shocked to see a two-story house with a separate garage standing in the forest where nothing had stood before. The new house seemed to have sprung up overnight. It was situated on the harbour northwest of us. I said, "I can't believe that a house and a garage like that were built in just a year."

"Yeah, it shows what changes a year can bring. Hope they're as nice as the Blacks," Maurie answered.

"It reminds me of a European home," I said. "Look at the high-peaked roofs...and the flower boxes. The buildings snuggle right into the forest."

"For just being built, their lawn and driveway really look good," Maurie remarked.

We noticed a long string of wooden stairs extending down the bank from the new house to a dock. A counter-weighted white ramp, which raised up and down with body weight, extended over the dock. Serenely floating alongside the dock was a beautiful sailboat.

We got the urge to go next door and introduce ourselves. A carved wooden sign hanging in the window to the right of the front door announced the name *Jos Van Meel.* "They must be Dutch," I whispered to Maurie, "that explains the style of the house."

Knock, knock. No answer. *Knock, knock.* Suddenly we heard footsteps rushing down from upstairs. A breathless woman greeted us at the door in her stocking feet. Her tall frame was imposing. The face was round with big pretty eyes. She grinned at us. "Yah, what can I do for you?"

"We're the Watsons," I said, "your neighbours next door. This is my husband Maurie and I'm Jackie. We came to say hello."

"How nice of you. My name is Thea Van Meel. You'll have to excuse me. I've been cleaning house." She stepped back and opened the door. "Won't you come in. But, first, please take off your shoes."

We stepped lightly over the threshold onto shiny wooden floors. White plaster walls backdropped old ornate furniture, an antique clock and heavily framed pictures. I looked beyond Thea and and saw a broad brick fireplace; large blue and white tiles painted with scenes of boats and windmills from Holland trimmed the hearth.

"Jos—my husband is at work," Thea said, "he's a contractor on the island."

"That explains how the house and garage were built so quickly," Maurie said. "Nothing was here last summer and building on the island takes a long time."

"Yah, that's for sure. We're from Vancouver and Jos came back and forth to work on the house."

"It's charming and you have such a wonderful view," I said.

"Thank you. There's also a bedroom and bath over the garage. Jos built that for Barbara, our daughter who comes to visit." Then Thea gestured at us. "I saw you cleaning the roof and gutters and climbing ladders. Don't you come up here to rest and be on vacation?"

We laughed. "When we're first here, it's all work," Maurie said, "you see, we're from San Diego and we rent the house most of the year. So we have to do repairs and clean things up. I'm flying back to San Diego to rest up from all this work. "

"Yah, but you'll be back?" Thea asked.

"Yes, in August," Maurie replied.

"You caught me unawares. Normally I'd have a pastry to offer you, but I've been cleaning."

We talked for a few minutes, then Maurie said, "We better go, Jacque. Thea, tell your husband to come by and see us when I return in August."

"Yah, I'll sure do that." There were two pairs of wooden shoes placed at the front door as we left.

"Do you really wear wooden shoes?" I asked.

"Oh, yah, they're called *klompen*. It's a Dutch habit. We wear *klompen* outside to work in the garden, then leave them at the front door when we come in. It keeps the house clean that way."

The neighbourhood was slowly developing. Marina Crescent Drive was paved and on our side of the road, there were the Van Meels, our house and the Blacks. The only dock in sight belonged to the Van Meels. The quality of our drinking water had improved, thanks to the successful efforts of the Scott Point Water Works in drilling more wells.

Maurie flew home to San Diego the next day, leaving me and the kids to fend for ourselves. But I felt comfortable. The Scotts had moved downstairs for a few weeks because their new house was not quite finished. The Blacks were nearby and Thea waved "Hello" every time I saw her.

◆◆◆

The Beachcomber occasionally chugged by in his work boat close to our bank. He alarmed me the first time he called out to us over his loud speaker.

"How's everything up there, Watsons?" His voice reverberated over the harbour. I ran out on our deck just in time to see the stern of his boat pass—full of driftwood and junk he picked up along the way. I saw his dog crawling around outside the boat. The boat continued to ply the water close to shore, then his loud speaker bellowed at the Blacks.

Kas ran right over to our house after the Beachcomber disappeared.

"Don't be surprised when that ol' Beachcomber comes by in his boat. He likes to shock people with his loud speaker."

"Well, he succeeded today," I said.

"I told you he's an odd one," Kas said. "He lives on that boat and does all kinds of jobs with it. He fishes. He beachcombs. He uses it to rescue other boats. Sometimes it's a water taxi."

"You got to hand it to him, though, he's very resourceful with what little he has," I said.

"I guess so. I hear that dog of his jumps off his boat to the dock carrying the bowline in his teeth and pulls the boat into the dock."

I laughed. "Smart dog."

Soon after that I noticed a broken water-ski was missing outside our carport.

10

ISLANDERS

My life and that of the house and the island actually started to merge in the summer of '75. Being alone with the kids for three weeks, I settled into island living. It felt like a real vacation. My body clock shifted from fast to slow. The pace slackened.

Sitting on the deck in early morning by myself with a cup of coffee and listening to the quiet became a simple pleasure. The sun rose over Nose Point cutting a golden path across the water, bathing our house with broad sunlight. The deep blue water was still and smooth. An occasional seagull, flapping its white wings, beelined by or suddenly dove into the water to catch a meal. Bird calls echoed across the harbour. Smoke curled lazily from a fisherman's cabin tucked out of view on a small, rocky island next to Maracaibo. Soon the fisherman's boat, the *Lady Jane*, emerged quietly from behind the rocks and headed toward open sea for a good day's work.

I watched time pass before my eyes. A gentle breeze came up later. Trees swayed, their branches waving as if to greet the pleasure boats floating by. Low tide exposed purple, pink and orange starfish clustered on the bank below. A red squirrel dashed across the railing, stopping momentarily and rising on his hind legs to chatter and beg for peanuts; then he jumped like an acrobat onto a nearby branch and waited for me to sprinkle his cache of peanuts on the railing. The ferry between Long Harbour and Tsawwassen churned slowly by a couple of times a day leaving gentle ripples in its wake.

In the late afternoon, the shores of Maracaibo, burnished with golden light, faded into the rocky shadows. The setting sun, like an ember, glowed at the end of the harbour behind black, silhouetted tree tops. As night fell, I looked up to the night sky, so clear, and saw millions of stars scattered to infinity. Only the dim reflection of Vancouver lights loomed above Maracaibo; a few cabin lights sparkled in the dark night. Waves gently slapped the shore. When the full moon shone, it was a spotlight illuminating nature's stage.

The children played for hours in the forest close to the house—a new experience for Southern California kids accustomed to palm trees and chaparral.

"Guess what, Auntie Jackie?" Lynn ran excitedly into the house followed by Scott and Charlotte. "There are two iddy-biddy trees growing outside by a big one."

"They're probably seedlings," I said. "That means those little trees have grown from seeds."

"Can we plant them somewhere?"

"Yeah, Mommie, we want to plant trees." Charlotte said.

"Well, let's take a look at these trees. To transplant them, you must carefully dig up all the roots," I told them.

So it was, that summer, that the kids and I tenderly moved two tiny balsam fir trees, diligently dug holes near the back steps and ceremoniously planted them.

"Each year, we'll come back to our house," I said, "and we'll see these little trees grow up, just like the three of you."

Getting acquainted with the islanders was an unexpected bonus. Along with making an investment in our house, I soon realized that I was making an investment in friends. I found islanders friendly and helpful. They were a special breed. Even though they were insular, self-sufficient and had detached from the rigors of big city living, the island made them dependent upon one another, closer, like people in a small town.

One friendship developed from reading an announcement in the *Gulf Islands Driftwood* newspaper.

"Loes Holland, certified tennis instructor for Island Parks and Recreation, will begin tennis classes for children next week. Sign up will be held at the tennis court by Mahon Hall next Tuesday from 10 A.M. to noon. Children must be accompanied by adults to schedule lessons."

"Hey, kids," I said, "how would you guys like to take some tennis lessons here this summer?"

"Yeah, that would be fun," Scott said, "then we could play with you."

The next Tuesday the kids and I drove to the tennis court near Mahon Hall, the only public court on the island. It looked a little sad. The gray, dried asphalt with faded white lines was surrounded by a chain-link fence, as old and mottled as tree bark. A group of parents, with children in hand, patiently stood around a tall, lanky lady in a tennis dress; her head, full of short white hair, stood above the crowd. A strong Dutch accent resonated in her high-pitched voice.

"Hallo, there," she said, looking at the kids. "Vould you like to take tennis lessons? Your mother must sign this list vid your name and phone number. Then I let you know when to come for lessons."

"Anytime will be fine," I said. "By the way, how do you pronounce your name?"

She laughed. "My first name is just like the vord, 'loose,' and our last name was so hard to say that my husband Gerry changed it to Holland before he arrived in Canada."

"Loes," I said, "I play tennis. Do you know anyone on the island who would like to play?"

"Yah, yah I love to play. And I know lots of people who do. Ve must have a game soon. I call you."

Loes and I began playing regularly. She seemed ageless; I never learned how old she was. The Hollands had come from Toronto, not long before us, to retire on the island.

"Ve stayed five months in the Blue Gables Resort near St. Mary's Lake while Wilf Bangert built our Holiday House," Loes told me.

"What's a Holiday House?" I asked.

"Oh, it's a pre-fab house, vere all the pieces are cut beforehand."

"We've got a pre-fab house too."

"Yah, yah. The only thing vas the boards vere delivered to the wrong place so ve paid ex-convicts to move the lumber up to the building site."

"Ex-convicts?"

"Yah, there vere ex-convicts being rehabilitated vere the Vesuvius Pub is and they moved the lumber in one day. Then ve had men from off the island do the electrical work, the dry wall, the plumbing. One of your American draft dodgers did the finishing vood vork. Gerry and I built the fireplace over eight months. A little cement every day and hiking in between. Ve carried the rocks in our packs when ve saw special ones."

Loes worked part-time as a radiographer in Lady Minto Hospital. Her enthusiasm for traveling was contagious.

"You know, last year I followed along the Silk Road, 9,000 miles" she said. "It was maaarvelous. Ve vent from Islāmābād to Beijing by plane and bus. I even rode a camel. Sometimes ve traveled by horse and wagon.

You've got to pack it all in and see the vorld before you get too old."

"Oh, I agree, Loes."

"I know all the hiking trails on the island. Vould you like to go on a little hike someday...vid the kids?"

"I haven't hiked for years."

"Ve could pack a little lunch and go to Ruckle Park."

"O.K., let's do it...someday."

The *Gulf Islands Driftwood* newspaper, published every Wednesday on Salt Spring and distributed to the other Gulf Islands, was a wonderful source of information. Editor Frank Richards, a white-haired, distinguished Englishman, discovered Salt Spring while stationed in Sidney with the RAF during World War II. He established his newspaper in 1966 and had a staff of three people—his wife, son and one of his daughters.

Mr. Richards' weekly paper gave all kinds of facts and figures. For example, I read that the island population was approximately 4,000. To my surprise some of the first settlers were African-Americans who migrated to Vancouver Island from California as early as 1859; several descendants were still living on the island. Early pioneer families hailed from Britain, Scotland, Ireland, Germany, Australia and Portugal. Hawaiians known as the Kanaka families settled on the island after working for the Hudson Bay Company. In early 1900 a Japanese family descended on the island to raise chickens and vegetables.

The newspaper touted Salt Spring lamb, considered a delicacy in the Vancouver-Victoria area and served by better restaurants to the immense satisfaction and the pride of the islanders. On another day, there was a charming lead article about hummingbirds, very important to the islanders, for as long as the mighty little birds fluttered and sucked nectar from flowers, warm weather would remain on the island.

Readers were well informed about the workings of B.C. government. Since the islands didn't have local government, they were governed by two authorities for the Gulf Islands—the Capital Regional District, known as the C.R.D., and the Islands Trust.

I was surprised to read that prior to 1965, there was only the "10-acre freeze" to regulate land development on the islands. During that year, the provincial government through legislation created seven regional districts throughout B.C. to control development. Each regional district was responsible for local services—sewers, hospitals, garbage disposal, parks, community planning, zoning, subdivisions and building inspection and was the financial authority for these functions. Salt Spring was represented by one C.R.D. director, who joined others from the Saanich Peninsula, Victoria and the western communities, to sit on the Capital Region board, which met in Victoria.

Then, in 1974, to further protect and preserve the islands through land use control, the Islands Trust was formed as a watchdog agency. The Gulf Islands were among 13 islands within the Strait of Georgia that fell in the Trust area. Two more Salt Spring representatives were elected to sit on the Trust Council. In the begin-

ning, the Islands Trust had neither administrative functions nor power; it approved or vetoed C.R.D. land-use
recommendations only. However, with the new Islands
Trust Act in 1990, the Island Trust took over planning,
zoning and building permits from the CRD.

Each Wednesday, I eagerly awaited the latest news.
Instead of pounding island drums for communication,
natives drove into Ganges to pick up the latest
Driftwood.

When a thundering blast came from the direction of
the Blacks' trailer, it alarmed me. I ran out to our road
to see what happened. Construction trucks were lined
along the property next door. A tall tree came crunch-
ing down. Men were busily clearing the underbrush.

Oh-oh, there must be a house going up. Being
inquisitive, I slowly walked down the road. A swarthy,
balding man with a dark beard appeared to be in charge.

"New house going in here?" I asked.

"Yes, we're preparing the site," the man answered.

"I understand someone by the name of Netboy owns
the property. I've never met him, " I said.

"That's right. I am his architect. My name is Hank
Schubart"

Migs had told me about Hank Schubart—that he was
the leading architect on the island.

"Hello," I said, extending my hand, "I'm Jackie
Watson. So nice to meet you. I understand you've
designed many houses on the island."

"Yes. About 100. I was the only architect here for years."

"And how long have you been on the island?"

"Since 1968. Why, all I needed to build in those days was a shovel and a 2x4. There were no building permits or controls." He turned to watch another tree being felled. "I only cut down trees when it's necessary. I study the site for days for it's the most important factor. I design a house so it fits organically into the surroundings."

I curiously watched the beginning construction, wondering how the finished home would appear. Later that summer I stepped into a Schubart-designed home on Long Harbour. The home nestled beautifully in the woods. Windows framed stunning vistas of landscape and waterscape; transoms, windows and skylights seemed to bring the forest into the house. I eagerly anticipated having a Schubart home next door.

Cyril and Carrie Louise were wonderful neighbours, always willing to be of help. "Thought I'd call and see how you all are doin," Carrie Louise said on the phone. "Listen, if you need any fresh vegetables or bread, I know just the lady for you to see."

"Hey, that sounds good. Who is she?" I asked

"Mrs. Wiedswang." Carrie Louise giggled a little.

"Weed...what?"

"W-I-E-D-S-W-A-N-G. Funny name. I think it's Norwegian. Anyway, she lives on a farm with her deaf husband. Call her first to see if she's home. Then go see all her yummy things."

"Hello, Mrs. Wiedswang?" I said on the phone.

"Yes, this is Mrs. Wiedswang," she answered. "What can I do for you?"

"I'd like to come to your farm and buy some vegetables and baked things."

"Fine. Come along. I just made blackberry pies this morning and I have a fresh batch of mustard beans. What time do you want to come over?"

"I'll be there at 3 o'clock this afternoon."

Discovering Mrs. Wiedswang was like discovering gold. In her garage-turned-pantry was a treasure-trove: beets and potatoes fresh from the ground, green beans and carrots snapping with flavour, lettuce still warm from the sun and brown eggs rich in taste. A rainbow of colourful jars covered a table: mustard beans, mustard pickles, crabapple jelly, blackberry jam, peach and mango chutney. Blackberry, blueberry, apple, rhubarb and raspberry pies were either freshly baked or frozen. To peer into her freezer full of cinnamon rolls, bran muffins, pecan tarts, zucchini bread and lemon pound cake was better than looking into a treasure chest.

The kids snickered over her name, calling her "Mrs. Wingwang" or "Mrs. Wigwam." When I returned home with food from her farm, everyone hungrily looked over my selections.   "Well, what did you get at Mrs. Whizbang's today?" Scott asked. (The children doubled up with laughter over his smart aleck name.)

"No, Scott," I said, "You got her name wrong...it's Mrs. Wig-Wag."

Going to Mrs. Wiedswang's became a delicious habit. She laboured year-round in her kitchen. "Even though I've got diabetes, you know, and don't feel so good some days, I've got to keep busy doing something," she said, "otherwise I'd go crazy."

Dennis and Carol Scott had to rent the downstairs suite for most of the summer; their house construction took longer than they thought. Such kind, considerate tenants—a refreshing change from the deranged doctor and family. We became fast friends, especially after Dennis offered us a freshly caught salmon.

When Maurie returned in August, he seemed pleased and content in the house. The lazy days melted one into another. Just after Maurie's return, there was a *tap-tap-tap* on our kitchen door. Thea stood on the deck, a short stocky man at her side. "Hallo, I'm Jos Van Meel," he said with a smile, "and I came to meet you."

"Come in, come in," Maurie said, "and we'll have a cup of coffee."

Jos had a kind face. He had blondish wavy hair and clear, sparkling blue eyes. Thea towered above him.

"Well, you have a nice place here," Jos said in heavily accented English. Thea followed him as he strolled toward the cathedral windows and gazed across the harbour. He turned and said to Maurie, "I saw your boat in the driveway."

"Yes, we pulled it and the trailer up here from San Diego. And it's the last time," Maurie answered. "I'm going to import the boat and leave it during the winter."

Along with the coffee, good feelings were brewed with the Van Meels. As we talked, I sensed they were glad to have us as neighbours.

"Where do you launch your boat?" Jos asked.

"We'll launch it at the end of the harbour," Maurie answered. "Then we keep it at the Cunninghams' dock near the launch."

"Well, now, why don't you leave your boat at our dock?" Jos suggested. "It would be easier for you just to walk down our stairs and get into your boat."

Maurie looked at me with a happy grin. "That's very kind of you. Are you sure that you don't mind having all of us traipse across your property?" Maurie asked.

"Not at all," Jos answered.

Thus, another friendship was forged. Jos and Thea became voluntary watchdogs and guarded the house in our absence. In the summertime, Thea occasionally brought a handful of Dutch pastries—it was like a handful of neighbourliness.

Loes kept the children busy with tennis lessons at the school court. When I dropped them off for their lesson one day, she came running up to the car full of excitement. "Vork has started at Central on the new tennis courts and the track. You know, vere Arthur and Joane Millner had their farm?"

"Great," I said, "maybe next year we'll have something decent to play on."

"Yah, yah. I've been on the Parks and Recreation Commission and have been pushing for more tennis courts. Gosh! It's been a lot of work. I've gone to 24 meetings of the parks and rec commission and I've given speeches to raise money."

"Really? Good for you."

"Ve're lucky. The Salt Spring Lions Club paid for the Millner property. But there still may be a referendum to raise more money."

Loes looked over her shoulder and saw kids hitting wild tennis balls around the court. "Vell, I better start their lesson now. Don't forget about our hike this veek"

Our hikes with Loes took us from Shepherd Hills to Maxwell Mountain. Along the way she pointed out wild rose bushes, forest ponds and Spanish moss. Her high-pitched chatter about the flora and fauna rose melodiously above the tree tops. She talked endlessly about people on the island. "You know," she said, "people think they're getting away vid things by coming to an island, but they don't."

"What do you mean?" I asked.

"Vell, there's lots of hanky-panky here. Ve should call Salt Spring Island—'Bedspring Island.' There are as many affairs nesting on the island as there are birds in the trees."

11

SEWER STINK

Beneath the village of Ganges, with its boxy, non-descript buildings, bubbled a real stench during low tide. The scent wafted up from antiquated holding tanks, septic tanks and gallons of effluent flowing into the harbour from the Ganges schools and hospital.

There was another stink, among the islanders, as to whether or not Ganges needed a sewer to take care of the problem. The issue got under people's skin. Riled them up. Made them hot and cranky, ready to fight: neighbour vs. neighbour, friend vs. friend. A typical example was a mother of three who said, "...It's divided our family. My husband and his old man don't talk anymore, that's how deep it runs." Hanging over all the controversy was the aroma off Ganges Harbour.

We first ran afoul of the issue in the summer of 1975. Another sewer proposal had been defeated by the opposition's furious appeal that the project "didn't meet standards."

"How," Maurie asked Cyril, "can a *sewer* get people so riled up?"

Cyril shrugged, spread his palms. "People have been arguing about the sewer since 1940," he said. "That was the year the Ganges schools started dumping raw sewage into the harbour, right next to the Ganges Marina."

"Which accounts for the smell, eh?" Maurie said.

"Yes," Cyril smiled. "Why, if the sewer had been built in 1940, when the Chamber of Commerce first proposed it, it would have only cost $180,000. To build a sewer today will cost $400,000."

The opponents of the sewer lined up with the Albertan French-Canadian Yvette Valcourt and her entrepreneurial husband Phil. The Valcourt family worked hard to develop a building supply outlet and a 21 unit shopping center on Lower Ganges Road, outside the Ganges core area. The island's first zoning laws were drawn by inexperienced planners and the community plan ignored expansion in the area where the Valcourts had business. They became frustrated when their property and three acres across the street were zoned as "residential," and "non-conforming commercial property." Feeling they had the right to prosper, they joined a segment of the community seething over these intrusions on private property rights. Yvette soon became spokesman for the opponents of planning. Along the way, there were clashes with the regional director and downtown merchants, namely Mouat's Trading Company Ltd.. Eventually the Valcourts received commercial zoning.

The spunky, outspoken Frenchwoman then took up the cause to fight the sewer, saying "a small group of self-interested people were acting under the guise of knowing what's best" for Ganges. She got herself elected director for the Capital Regional District (C.R.D.) which managed the pursestrings and permits for projects such as the Ganges sewer. Islanders and members of the liberal New Democratic Party rallied behind the formidable Valcourt as she aggressively thwarted the sewer development through appeals and court cases.

The Ganges Sewer Committee, appointed by the Ganges Chamber of Commerce, valiantly struggled against these adversaries. Frank Richards, the editor of the *Gulf Islands Driftwood*, was chairman of the committee; Richards owned no property at the time and was only concerned with eliminating "the stink." Richards told the story about his London visitor who was strolling with Frank through Ganges one day when the smell was up. His visitor wrinkled her nose and asked, "What's that filthy smell?"

And Richards replied, "Well, that's Ganges. That's why we're trying to get a sewer."

"Sewer? Do you mean DRAINS?" the visitor asked. "Do you mean to say you have a town this size that doesn't have DRAINS?"

Richards claimed the visitor swore never to come back to the island.

Other members of the Sewer Committee were Jim Wilkinson, a Valcourt supporter, and Tom Toynbee of Mouat's Trading Company. Toynbee had a vision for the community and told islanders that the Ganges sewer was a necessary part of the community plan, but he was accused of wanting the sewer to promote Mouat's Trading Company and to help "a few downtown developers." The conservative Social Credit Party backed the sewer proposal.

Attacks came flying from both sides, emotions ran high.

Valcourt and opponents bitterly criticized Toynbee for being part of the "ol' boy network" and accused him of using his position as Chairman of the Housing Corporation of British Columbia in an unethical manner to further his own business interests. Toynbee counter-attacked with a letter to the C.R.D. asking for an investigation of Yvette Valcourt's use of her office to stifle development in shopping areas other than her own property.

A large number of islanders were against dumping effluent through the outfall pipe into the harbour. Some residents living along the harbour believed without a doubt that an outfall pipe would bring even more stink. Other islanders wanted a sewer with effluent used as water on the hillsides. Environmentalists clamored for alternatives to a sewer, such as; building a sand-filtration plant outside Ganges or redirecting sewage into Sansum Narrows.

Finally, by an act of the B.C. legislature in 1981, the provincial government decreed the sewer be built and have connections to the hospital and the Ganges schools. The installation of the outfall pipe started in July, 1981.

In August, 1981, when we were vacationing on the island and after the installation of the outfall pipe began, the sewer saga really got rough. Cyril stopped by to bring us apples from his tree. "Did you hear what happened in the harbour last night?"

"No, what?" Maurie asked.

"When I was working at Mouat's this morning, I heard a quarter-million dollars worth of plastic pipe was burned."

"You mean sewer pipe?"

"Yes. The pipe was aboard a barge and had just been delivered yesterday. I understand there was a barrel of fuel aboard too. If that had caught fire, the whole thing would have blown to smithereens. Sounds like the contractor will be responsible for the cost of the pipe, and depending upon his insurance, he may have to pay up."

"Geez, who do you think did it?"

"Who knows. Rumor has it that arsonists did it. But it remains a mystery."

Then, in December, 1981, more destruction, and a *second* fire. Cyril sent us the story from the *Driftwood:*

> "...during the continued progress of the work (on the sewer), one of the guard dogs was shot and the construction equipment on an unattended barge was destroyed in a second fire of undetermined origin...

The work has been carried out in 'exem-
plary fashion' and has been completed
within the specified date despite the fire,
threats and harassment which were report-
ed by the engineering department..."

It's getting dangerous when guard dogs are shot. I
thought as I put the newspaper clipping down. *There are
some real zealots on that island.* How the two fires
were started remained a mystery.

Opponents were relentless. After almost all of the
outfall pipe was laid at a cost of nearly $2 million, they
demanded the C.R.D. put a moratorium on the construction of the sewage treatment plant. The reason?
The plant would cost more than estimated and should be
redesigned to meet original estimates.

The situation moved a Victoria newspaper to edito-
rialize: IS IT REALLY SEWERCIDE? The article stated, "In the words of the local paper, the *Driftwood*, 'The
consensus tends to assign responsibility for the fire to
opponents of the sewer project.'" The article wondered
if the provincial government would use its power to
counteract Valcourt and the anti-sewer allies on the
C.R.D. who were expected to deny funds *already
approved* for the sewage treatment plant.

However, Bill Ritchie, Minister of Municipal
Affairs, who was about to retire, came to the rescue by
ordering a special grant to help complete the sewage
treatment plant in 1986. Yvette Valcourt lost her position on the C.R.D. for protecting her interests. The
Valcourts eventually disposed of their holdings on Salt
Spring and retired to Victoria.

What started out to be a $400,000 project twenty years before, ended up costing $4,000,000.

Approximately 140 properties in the common area of Ganges, the hospital and the Ganges Schools were hooked up to the sewer. The future looked bright for Ganges and for the harbour. But, feelings still smoldered, bitterness remained, and the passion left scars for years.

A quote from a Victoria newspaper summarized the 20 years of the sullied sewer situation:

> "It's paradise here," rejoined a customer paying   for lunch in a cafe. "There ain't no snake here. So, it's like this, we made one out of the sewer. It's going to be the best sewer on the coast— but in this Eden it's become a snake in the garden."

12
FORGETTING CARES
OF THE WORLD

My parents felt comfortable on Salt Spring, knowing our island friends. After trading in the shops for supplies and hardware to repair our house, Ganges village was like hometown to them. Butchart Gardens and Victoria became their favourite haunts off-island. Dad was a ham radio operator so he set up his small radio rig in our house and broadcast to all the islands and the mainland; as a result, he had friends on the air from Salt Spring, the Saanich Peninsula and around the Strait of Georgia.

Loving the island as they did, Mom and Dad wanted my uncle Jimmie Reinert, mother's youngest brother, and my aunt Marion to join them on a driving trip up there in the spring of '76; the four of them were close and enjoyed many vacations together. The upstairs level was rented, however the downstairs suite could comfortably accommodate four people. And so, the two couples, who both lived in Orange County, climbed in Dad's roomy Cadillac and meandered slowly north, stopping at scenic spots in Oregon and Washington along the way.

It pleased me to imagine my parents enjoying our house and all its pleasures; it especially pleased me that they wanted to share our house with Jimmie and Marion. In a way, I was envious when they left—knowing they would see spring unfold its panoply of colours in a montage of rhododendrons, daffodils, dogwood and azaleas.

We didn't hear from them. Then, after they were gone a few weeks, there was a phone call from Carrie Louise.

"Honey," she said, "Bud wanted me to call you and let you know they've packed up the car and are headin' home early with Jimmie and Marion."

"Why did they leave early?" I said surprised and puzzled. "Weren't they having a good time up there?"

"Yes, they were havin' a wonderful time, but Helen started not feeling so well this last week," Carrie answered. "She had trouble eating and seemed kinda sick to her stomach. In fact, we had everybody for dinner the other night and she could hardly eat a thing."

'Geez, that doesn't sound so good. I wonder what the trouble is. But thanks for calling, Carrie. I'll probably hear from them when they get home."

I hung up the phone feeling disappointed that their trip was cut short by another of my mother's complaints. She seemed to always have some kind of ailment. I suspected she had a streak of hypochondria. And my father, a healthy, happy man, babied her. He glossed over her problems. I knew why he put Carrie up to calling me because he avoided difficult situations; he didn't want to face telling me she was sick again.

I visited Mother after they returned to Orange County. She looked all right, so I wasn't alarmed. Like so many times before, the doctor couldn't diagnose the problem. When it came time for us to leave for Canada that summer, I had no reservations about going. *She'll soon get over this*, I thought to myself.

Arriving on the island was exciting. Cyril dropped by to invite us for dinner the first night. "It's so good to see you back," Cyril said. "Carrie Louise has been working in the kitchen roasting a leg of Salt Spring lamb and baking a pecan pie just for you." Kas marched over to our house the next day with bags of fresh vegetables and her homemade bread. Being on Salt Spring chased our cares away; we relaxed and eased into our favourite pastimes. Like collecting driftwood. And going to Walker Hook.

It really was a hook—a hook of land jutting out on the northeast side of Salt Spring on the Trincomali Channel. Mother Nature carved it with wind and tides. Inside the hook, on low tide, the receding water left a swampy marsh full of reeds. At the northeast tip of the hook was a line of rocks parallel with the shore and word had it that scallops and abalone resided in the water at 15 meters. Sandstone rocks, supporting trees and bushes, formed the outside of the hook—a good place to climb and to poke in tidepools.

Coming by boat, loaded with sand buckets, towels, and a picnic lunch, we landed on the southeast side of the hook, our favourite side. We rolled in on shallow, warm waves, beached our boat, then tied the bow line to a heavy piece of driftwood, knowing the shore was shallow and not good for mooring. The hook was connected to the island by a long, curving beach; inside the curve light-green sea lettuce drifted in and out with the tide; beyond the curve stands of trees backed the beach. A scattering of shells and small rocks, exposed along the water's edge, lined the shore. The scent of the sea touched our noses, gentle breezes brushed our faces and sea water encircled our feet. Just a few souls wandered on this quiet beach. We spread out our towels over the warm sand and comfortably sat, dreamily viewing the misty-blue islands in the distance.

Driftwood, like silver skeletons, typically collected on the beaches and coves of the Northwest, but Walker Hook was an extraordinary catch-all. Powerful winter tides carried driftwood of all sizes to this beach—huge logs, uprooted trunks, smaller sculpted pieces, worm-eaten cedar—and piled it high on the upper shore. The wood, stripped of bark and soaked in salt water, glistened in the sun.

I spent hours climbing on the driftwood—balancing myself with arms thrust outward—wearing only a bathing suit and tennis shoes. The warmth of the sun seeped into my back. With deep concentration, forgetting the world around me, I poked and prodded for gray-twisted treasures. In between the massive trunks, I found dried strands of dark seaweed, bleached shells and debris. To my delight, I uncovered a unique piece of driftwood with angles and curves, with worm holes, with such character that it had to be taken back to the boat.

The children—their sand buckets next to them—dug holes in the wet shore searching for shells. Unconcerned with the gritty sand coating their arms and their legs, they intensely shoveled. In the distance, Maurie stood on the rocks, arms crossed, and gazed out at the Trincomali Channel—he wore his favourite white boat hat turned down over his ears. a white t-shirt and old swimming trunks.

Feeling hungry, I called across the beach, "How about a swim before lunch?"

"Yeah, yeah, let's do it," yelled the kids, "the last one in is a donkey's tail."

Surprisingly, the British Columbia water in small coves and along shallow shores was quite warm in the summertime. We splashed around, refreshing ourselves with a swim. With healthy appetites, we devoured our lunch, then lay like sleepy lizards under the afternoon sun. It was a perfect time to read, to sleep, to rest.

In the afternoon, when the sun's angle filtered through the trees and the air cooled, we collected our sandy gear, priceless driftwood, buckets of shells and climbed in the boat.

"Hey, hey, that's enough driftwood in the boat," Maurie reprimanded us, "there won't be any room left for you to ride home." We reluctantly left a few pieces on the shore.

Heading back toward Nose Point, I braced myself against the wind and waves, feeling exhilarated. A day at Walker Hook was like taking "time out" from life; a time to soak up the sun and sea; to make play our day's work.

North of Walker Hook, along a bank near the water, the biggest, mouth-watering blackberries grew. In the heat of August, the berries sweetened under the sun. The entangled wild vines were loaded, just waiting to be picked.

There was a certain technique to successful berry-picking. I hung a empty, plastic ice cream bucket over my arm to collect the berries. To really get into the bushes without the thorns scratching my skin, I wore old, long pants and Maurie's long-sleeved, frayed shirts; even then the prickles snagged my clothing and made it difficult to move. My head was protected by a hat or visor— otherwise my face became so scratched I looked like I'd come out of a cat fight.

The berries were sweet and fragile in contrast to their thorny vines. Berries hanging just out of reach, untampered, grew big and succulent; they dangled in the distance, tempting me to reach beyond my grasp. Some were hiding behind a leaf, easily picked and thrown in the bucket. Occasionally a plucked berry would burst between my fingers—the juice dribbling down my arm, under my cuff, staining skin and cloth a deep, sweet violet.

Once, we took the kids and four house guests to the same patch on the bank just after a rain. The berries looked especially tantalizing—sparkling fresh from the rain. Our friend Bill Emery spotted some big berries in the middle of the patch and called out, "Hey, I've found some of the biggest berries I've ever seen—they're glimmering, just waiting to be picked."

He stood on his tip-toes, stretching forward and balancing his bucket at the same time. Suddenly the rain-soaked earth gave way beneath him and he disappeared under the berry patch somewhere down the bank.

"Whoaa," came his pitiful cry. Some awful tumult echoed from underneath the patch. "Ouch, this hurts like hell," he yelled. "Somebody help me, I'm caught."

We carefully crawled around the berry patch, slipping down the muddy bank. At the bottom of the bank, short of the water line, Bill hung in delicate balance snagged in the back by a big bramble. Streams of blood and berry juice trickled down his head; his clothes were muddy and torn. He looked like beat-up puppet on a string and he was MAD. "Damn it," he snarled, "just don't stand there staring at me. Somebody get me unhooked from this mess!"

But the scrapes on the body and berry stains on clothing were worth it. Even the purple berry stains in the kitchen were worth it; in the kitchen, we washed, trimmed and transformed buckets of blackberries into pies, cobblers and ice cream toppings. And a big bowl of blackberries for breakfast or mixed with cereal started the day in grand style. One of our house guests was so crazy about the blackberries, she froze bags of berries and flew home with them.

Not Bill, though. "It was a berry too far," he said. His appetite for berries was left on the muddy bank that rainy afternoon. He left his berries there, too.

Another favourite pastime, especially Maurie's, was crabbing. He stood fascinated on the Van Meels' dock peering into the crab-rich waters. The red rock crabs, crawling on the underwater rocks, were smaller than the Dungeness but had bigger, meatier claws. It was more difficult to pick the meat from the rock crab, but it was just as sweet and delicious.

Maurie prepared his gear and went into his crab-catching routine whose success was the envy of our neighbours. He baited a large, plastic trap shaped like a criss-crossed beehive. Fish heads or trimmings from rock cod provided the bait—they were tied with wire inside the trap. An opening with pliable plastic fingers on top of the beehive allowed the crab to climb in, but prevented him from climbing out.

Maurie tossed the trap out into the water from the dock with a rope trailing behind. When the trap settled on the rocky bottom, he tied the rope to the dock for overnight. The next morning, he said, "I'm going to check the crab trap. Hope we have some keepers." (A "keeper" was a male crab measuring 115 mm. across the body—about equal to the size of a man's hand.)

"I'll put the crab pot on to boil and then I'll join you," I told him.

He pulled up the rope and raised the trap clear of the dark-green water. Crabs frantically clawed the sides, trying to escape. A large, orange starfish in the shape of a sunburst made a nuisance of its ugly self by sprawling across the opening; thousands of its tiny curlicue tentacles were trying to reach the bait.

"I'll get rid of you, Mr. Sunburst, muy pronto," Maurie said as he flung the the horrid thing in the water.

He looked inside the trap and exclaimed with delight, "Hey, we got some beauties with big claws. I'll measure them to make sure they're keepers."

With a big smile, he said, "Look at this big one." He proudly held up a very large crab with his fingers just behind its front claws—which were pinching dangerously in the air. Maurie sorted out the crabs by measuring them on a lined piece of wood. He threw the smaller crabs and females back into the water. On the dock, he split each body in two pieces with an axe head, twisted off the claws, rinsed everything in salt water, and put the pieces in an old bucket; he never took more crab than we could eat.

The crab pot was boiling when we brought the catch up to the house. It took ten minutes to boil crab...and several hours to clear the air of the lingering crab smell in the house. But, it was all worth it, for after the crab was cold, came the time to crack it.

Cracking crab was a social event in our house. Our dining room table was covered with newspaper, bowls, forks and pickers. Maurie cracked the crab with a hammer and pliers while our house guests, the kids and I patiently picked the white morsels of meat from the legs and body; the claws held large lumps of meat and were easiest to clean. Each of us had a bowl for the crab meat—there were larger communal bowls for the shells. We picked the meat, then tossed the shells into the larger bowls. It was like being in a seafood restaurant—the heavy crab smell hung over our heads and the chatter was constant. We dipped the crab meat in melted butter or cocktail sauce, ate it with French bread or saltine crackers and chased it with beer or wine.

"Ummm, delicious!" Maurie said, butter dripping off his chin onto his bib—the bib read, "I've got the best legs in the house."

The summer passed too quickly. A contractor with reputable references was ready to rent our house. When we held our Mexican party, it signaled that we would soon leave the island. The Cunninghams, the Blacks, the Van Meels, the Hollands, Migs and her daughter Janet, the Beckmanns and others joined in the fun; the tequila and tacos seemed to top off the summer. During that evening, Loes insisted, "You must come to our house for supper before you leave."

It was always a treat to be invited to dinner by Loes and Gerry. Their house, perched atop Trincomali Heights, was like being on top of the world—it over-looked the Trincomali Channel, Galiano, Wallace Island and the Secretary Islands. At sunset, a rosy haze lingered over the islands and slowly faded late into the night. Loes spoiled us with her Dutch cooking—with flavours deliciously foreign to us. Our dessert course was a surprise—an exotic pastry made by Gerry, the baker in the family.

With dinner finished and a few drops of wine left in our glasses, Loes started bubbling about the new tennis courts and track.

"Aren't the two new courts vonderful?"

"Quite an improvement over that old school court," I agreed.

"I'm so glad the referendum passed to finish Portlock Park, that's vat it will be called, you know, in honour of Tommy Portlock who vorked on parks and rec. He's dead now."

"Will there be more courts eventually?" I asked.

"Yes, ve're planning for six. Ve just had the opening of the two courts last month in July, you know."

Our conversation was interrupted by the phone ringing.

"Hallo," answered Loes. "Oh, hallo, it's so nice to hear your voice. How are you?" She whispered to me, "It's your father."

"Yes, she's here. Ve just finished dinner. Vould you like to talk vid her?" Loes handed the phone to me.

"Hi, Dad. How ya doin'?" I asked.

"I'm fine," the tone of his voice sounded solemn. "But your mother is not good. That's why I'm calling. She's very sick."

I had forgotten all about her...about her "illness." The island, the relaxation, the good times had wiped her from my mind. But this time apparently she wasn't kidding. I felt suddenly, strangely scared.

"What about her doctor?" I asked. "What does he say?"

"He's done all he can do. He thinks she should see a specialist or go to a clinic. I really don't know where to turn."

All of my old resentment over her hypochondria disappeared in a flash of guilt. *I should be home with them, helping them, right now.* "Just a minute, Dad. Hold on." Anxiety set in, my mouth was dry.

I quietly said to Maurie, "Mother's still sick. Sounds like she's gotten worse. Dad doesn't know what to do...maybe see a specialist or take her to a clinic."

Maurie paused before answering, "I know a specialist at Scripps Clinic. Here, let me talk to your dad." I turned the phone over to Maurie.

"Hi Bud," Maurie said, "Listen, there's a Dr. Lee Schultz at Scripps Clinic in San Diego. He's an excellent doctor and a client of mine. Call him and make an appointment as soon as you can. I'm sure Lee can find out what's wrong with Helen. We'll leave the island tomorrow and be in San Diego as soon as we can."

The weeks that followed became a vigil. Dr. Schultz gave Mother a myriad of tests, then determined he should perform exploratory surgery. He discovered cancer in her pancreas—cancer, he told us, that was terminal—nothing could be done to help her.

During the weeks of her recovery from the surgery, Dad lived with us. He and I visited her daily in the hospital— gloom hung over us. Then, came the day when the hospital could no longer keep her.

"You better find a nursing home for her," Dr. Schultz told me. "I recommend that you take her back to Orange County where she can be near her family and friends during her final days."

"But *we are* her family...here in San Diego, doctor," I argued.

"I know, but I still think she would be more comfortable close to home where her friends can visit her," he insisted.

Dad and I took Mother by car and checked her into a nursing home in Orange County. In less than one week, she died from complications of pneumonia.

Her death stirred waves of guilt within me.

"If I hadn't gone to the island," I confessed to Maurie, "maybe she'd be alive today."

"Don't blame yourself," he said. "She was terminal."

"Yeah, she was terminal because I didn't get her into see a specialist like I should have. I was disgusted with her. I really didn't think she was that sick. I thought it was just another one of her complaints."

"It's not your fault."

"Oh, yes it is. I did all the wrong things. I wasn't attentive to her when the cancer started. I didn't want to move her to Orange County and I did. It was the trip that killed her!" And I started to cry.

13

THE ALBATROSS

It was fortunate we had a reliable tenant on the island that year for I couldn't think of much, except my mother's death and helping Dad sort out her belongings. I suffered from contradictions about her. She was gone, never to return, and I missed her dearly. Yet I had resented her illnesses while she was alive. She helped me, unstintingly, lovingly, whenever I needed her, like with the island house. Yet I was not there for her when cancer was germinating within her body. Sometimes, my grief was overwhelming.

Then, there was Dad dealing with his mourning. He came to San Diego frequently, arriving with such a forlorn look and suffering from loneliness. I remember how he sat at our kitchen table and wept. I never told him about my own guilt—the feeling I hastened Mother's death. We didn't discuss our feelings. Instead, I reminisced about the happy days of when I was growing up.

Following Mother's death at the end of the summer, we finished a renovation of a small Spanish-style house overlooking San Diego Bay and moved our family there in time for Thanksgiving. Many finishing touches remained to be done. I tried to keep Dad occupied by putting his mechanical talents to use.

"Dad, could you help Maurie put up some outdoor lights I bought in Tijuana?" I asked him. "Each one is wired differently."

"Here," he answered, "let me take a look at them. It will take some time, but I can figure each one out." Then he smiled and complained in a mocking way, "Someday I'd like to be invited to San Diego as a guest, not as a handyman."

Scott and Charlotte, who had become adolescents, added spice to Dad's life. True to his penchant for cars, Dad started looking for another old car when Scott got his driver's license. He found a used Plymouth in Orange County, brought it to San Diego and the two of them spent hours with their heads under the hood tinkering and tuning.

Taking Dad into consideration when the time came to make plans for Canada, we asked him to come with us and stay as long as he wanted. He was pleased and suggested, "You know, your mother and I enjoyed cruises so much, I'd like to go on a cruise to Alaska while I'm up there. Could Charlotte go with me?"

"Yeah, yeah, Grandpa," Charlotte piped up, "I'd love to see Alaska."

We drove in tandem to Vancouver—Dad in his Ford Ranchero, the rest of us in our station wagon. We put Dad and Charlotte aboard the ship—then headed for Tsawwassen to catch the late ferry to the island.

The one-week cruise lifted Dad's spirits—and taught Charlotte how to play bingo and bet on the horses. They came to the island full of tales about calving icebergs, pods of porpoise and eagles swooping to catch salmon. However, after a few days on the island, Dad's melancholy returned. He stood for hours on our deck by himself gazing at the harbour and smoking a cigarette—his private thoughts curling into the air like the smoke. Did the island dredge up bittersweet memories? Did it bring back the good times? I never asked him.

The summer had a different feeling. There was crabbing, berry-picking, fishing, socializing with island friends, tennis... and sadness lurking in the background. I was surprised when Dad asked, "Would you mind if I stayed on the island after you leave for San Diego? I'd like to be here for the fall...have a change of scenery. Maybe I could find a tenant for you then."

"Sure, Dad, stay, if you want," I answered. "Getting a tenant would be a big help. The Cunninghams and the Blacks would love to have you around. Besides, I have a list of repairs for you to do up here too."

He laughed. "You and your repairs."

The first snow fall dusted the island in late October. That was the signal for Dad to leave. He listed our house for rent in the *Driftwood* and I think he rented it to the first man to walk through the door.

"Found you a tenant, " Dad called on the phone. "He's British, young and seems very nice. He's the only one to answer the *Driftwood* ad and he's anxious the rent the house."

"Hmmm." I answered with misgivings. "Does he understand that he's to rent the place from November 1 until August 1 when we come up to use the house?"

"Yep. He has the rental money all ready for you. His name is Mr. J. Haddon."

It all sounded fine. A few months passed without incident, then the phone rang. Our neighbour Thea Van Meel was on the line. Her tone sounded disturbed. "I just had to call you because you should see the driveway and the carport at your house!"

"What's the matter, Thea?" I asked.

"Well, your tenant has put enough logs and wood in the driveway to build fires for five years."

"But he's only staying 'til August," I replied.

"I dunno. He looks settled in for while. The carport is a junkyard—cartons piled with debris, more wood, an old rusty bicycle, hoses, wires, dead plants and a broken lawnmower... it's disgraceful," our fastidious Dutch neighbor exclaimed. "Did you know he's living with a dark-haired woman too?"

"No, we didn't know anyone else was living in the house." *I hope we don't have more difficult tenants like that doctor and his wife.* "I'll call him and talk with him. Thanks, Thea, for letting us know."

I called Mr. Haddon and asked him to clean up the mess. I didn't mention that I knew he had a live-in because I had a hunch it would be useless. He claimed that the property was not cluttered and that our neighbour was nosy.

A month later we received a letter from Haddon.

> Dear Mr. and Mrs. Watson,
>
> I have great plans for your Canadian house. First, I want to move the carport down the driveway to create a patio for sunning in the afternoon. In the winter, the only sun is on the south side and a patio would be warm and secluded.
>
> Secondly, I want to cut out a window at the far end of the living room for a better view down the harbour. The dark cedar paneling would lighten up if another window were in the room.
>
> I'd be happy to get some estimates and employ the contractors to do the improvements for you.
>
> I anxiously await your reply.
> Sincerely,
> J. Haddon

I was furious after reading the letter. I shuddered at the thought of cutting a hole at the end of the living room for a window and moving the carport away from the house for a patio.

He acts like he owns the place.

I wrote him a letter stating we didn't wish to make his suggested improvements. I informed him that we were flying to Canada in the spring to celebrate the Cunninghams' 50th wedding anniversary, wanted to meet him and planned to inspect the premises.

He wrote that we must meet him at the Vancouver Airport because he was working on the mainland and renting an apartment there as well.

I bet he's avoiding seeing the property with us.

Unfortunately Maurie was detained by business and I had no choice but to fly to Vancouver to meet Haddon by myself. I felt uneasy.

In the airport I waited at the information desk where we were to meet. Then I saw a slender, dark-haired young man approaching me. He walked with determination; his eyes were piercing.

"You must be Mr. J. Haddon," I said, extending my hand. His hand felt like a cold fish. "So you work on the mainland?" I asked.

"Yes, it was more convenient for me to meet you here," Haddon answered. "Have you reconsidered my proposals for your house? I have it all figured out what we can do and I would be happy to supervise the construction for you."

"Mr. Haddon, let's take first things first." I tried to be firm. "Our neighbour still complains about the mess in the carport and the driveway. You must clean that up. I plan to inspect the premises while I'm on the island."

"It's not a mess. I just have accumulated a few things there. But back to your house—it has so much potential for improvement..."

I interrupted him. "Mr. Haddon, we don't have the money for your suggestions and we don't want to make any changes with the house."

Haddon stuck his chin out and glared at me like a child not getting his way. "All right, Mrs. Watson, if that's what you want, we have nothing more to discuss." He turned abruptly and started walking away.

"Please remember you must vacate the house by August 1," I called after him, wondering if he would honor our agreement.

I went on to the island to celebrate the Cunninghams' 50th wedding anniversary. Migs brought her new husband Wes Edwards to the party. Wes was a retired American who owned a home on the north end of the island called Southey Point. The couple resided there, however Migs retained her interests in Maracaibo with the plan of building someday.

After the anniversary celebration, I inspected the outside of our house when I was sure Haddon was not on the premises. I agreed with Thea—the driveway and carport looked like a pig sty. Yet, I knew after dealing with the Kensington-Smythes, there was little I could do about it.

Kas Black called me in San Diego—the tone of her voice was foreboding.

"Your tenant Haddon and his girlfriend are sunbathing on lounge chairs on the roof of the carport. Archie says the legs of the lounge chairs are damaging the roof."

I had a strange sinking feeling in my stomach. More problems.

"And he's brought an extension cord from the house out to the driveway where he plugs it into a typewriter. There he sits in his bathing suit on sunny days typing to his heart's content."

"We'll call him about the lounge chairs, Kas, but it won't do much good. As for the typewriter and extension cord, he's not hurting anything."

"They're weird. Did you know a covered mattress with two pillows are in the driveway? The two of them lay there and look like they're fornicating. Archie nearly ran his car in the ditch when he saw the hanky-panky. I hope you'll get them out of there in August."

Oh, Geez, that's all we need in the driveway.

Maurie phoned Haddon. "Mr. Haddon, our neighbours tell us you're keeping lounge chairs on the carport roof for sun bathing. Is this true?"

"Yes, Mr. Watson," Haddon answered. "Since you won't let me move the carport to make a patio for sunning, putting lounge chairs on the roof is the only way I can get some sun."

"That will damage the roof, Mr. Haddon, so remove them immediately."

"I'm sorry, Mr. Watson, but there's not much you can do about the lounge chairs since you live so far away."

"That doesn't mean you can do what you damn well please with our property. Remove them, Mr. Haddon! Also, I understand you keep a mattress in the driveway..."

There was a resounding "click." Haddon hung up.

"I have bad feelings about Haddon," I confided to Maurie. "Do you think he'll leave by August 1? Should we go to Canada as we plan this summer?"

"Absolutely! We gotta get rid of that guy, even if we have to take legal steps to do it."

There was no July rental check. Haddon felt like an albatross around our necks.

The family, Dad and the dog all went to the island at the end of July. Charlotte and I rode to Seattle with Dad in his car and picked up our puppy labrador who was flown to the SeaTac Airport. We proceeded by ferry to Swartz Bay, then met Maurie and Scott who flew into Victoria Airport. Our family, crowded in Dad's car, landed on the island August 1. The car stopped short in the driveway—the mattress was still there. Behind the mattress lay more junk. Lounge chairs were still on the roof.

Maurie sighed. "Christ, what a mess. I hate confronting this bastard. It's like fighting with that first tenant, that doctor, Kensington-Smyth all over again."

Maurie walked slowly to the back door and we trudged behind him. When he knocked, Haddon opened the door, his eyes blazing. He blurted out, "Even though it's August 1, we're not moving, Mr. Watson, and you can't trespass on the property without my permission."

By him stood a frail woman with long black hair; her flowing gingham dress trimmed with lace looked almost ethereal. Her large dark eyes were glazed.

"We have tenants' rights, we have tenants' rights," she insisted, her soft voice floating away into the air.

I bet she's on drugs.

"Tenants' rights or not, you're not honoring our rental agreement," Maurie said. "This is our property and you're not telling us what to do with it. You were to be out of here by August 1." Maurie by nature was a mild-mannered man but when angered, he unleashed words that cut anyone down to size. "You're leaving, Mr. Haddon. If you don't cooperate, we'll legally move you out. Until then, we'll be in the downstairs suite planning your exit."

The five of us were cramped downstairs; the dog howled in the dark night. Dad soon moved to the Cunninghams and we flew Scott home with the dog after two weeks.

The vacation turned into a war—downstairs versus upstairs. Our strategy was to make life miserable for Haddon and his girlfriend. We climbed on the roof to sweep the leaves and clean the gutters leaving dirty debris on Haddon's upper deck. For several days Maurie and Dad used a sander that made an unbearable noise grinding away old red paint from the upstairs and downstairs decks; the red dust coated the windows and railings.

The enemies' maneuvers tried our patience. Every sunny day Haddon and his roommate lolled on lounge chairs on the carport roof and didn't allow us to inspect the upstairs quarters. He sat on a stool in the driveway like an Indian prince wearing his tribal bathing suit continuously typing as if doing a ritual to the Sun God. The mattress remained in the driveway forcing us to step over it to go to and from the downstairs suite.

Haddon and his girlfriend disappeared to the mainland periodically, giving us peace in their absence. It appeared he didn't have a regular job. When they returned to the island, they sequestered themselves in the house, except to sunbathe. We never saw them using the mattress, thank goodness.

The battle raged on.

"This situation is so bad that I've made an appoint-ment with a rentalsman in Victoria, " Maurie said.

"What's a rentalsman?" I asked.

"It's a government employee who mediates disputes between landlord and tenants. We can find out the land-lord-tenant laws of British Columbia and maybe the rentalsman can help us get rid of Haddon."

The huge government building in Victoria loomed before us. After walking through a labyrinth of offices, we were directed to the desk of Elizabeth Baker. She was a large, blonde woman with an Australian accent. Miss Baker listened to our story. I was impressed by her professional manner.

"Mr. and Mrs. Watson, unfortunately the landlord-tenant laws favor the tenants in British Columbia. Damaging the carport roof and cluttered premises aren't enough grounds to remove Mr. Haddon."

Oh, this sounds familiar. Sounds like Kensington-Smyth all over again.

"How about not paying the rent?" Maurie asked.

"That's a possibility. How many months hasn't he paid?"

"He hasn't paid for July. Since he continues to live in our house, he should pay the August rent—he hasn't paid that either."

Elizabeth Baker leafed through a book on her desk and looked up thoughtfully.

"If he doesn't pay the rent for two months and if we can have a hearing at your house with neighbours testi-fying as to the misuse of the premises, perhaps there might be a case against him, but a weak one."

"Our neighbours will gladly testify," I said, "they want him out of there too."

Stopping at a page in her book and reading it intensely, Elizabeth Baker suggested, "There's another way to remove him, but it would be costly to you."

"How?" I asked.

"You say your father is here with you and that he was recently widowed? Since he's fairly free, would he be willing to stay in your house?

"Yes," I replied.

"For a year?" Miss Baker asked.

"A year?" I swallowed hard.

"Precisely."

"We'd receive no rental money?" Maurie asked.

Miss Baker pointed her finger at us. "I told you it would be costly."

Maurie shrugged his shoulders. "How would that work?"

"By law, you can terminate a tenant's right to rent your property if a family member is going to use the premises for at least a year."

Maurie and I looked at each other. "Do you think Dad would be willing?" I asked Maurie. He frowned and didn't reply. *He doesn't want Dad to do that.*

Miss Baker left the idea for us to consider and set a date for a hearing on the island in two weeks. She advised that a notice for rental payment be posted on Haddon's door when we returned to the island. We shook hands with Miss Baker and started to leave her office.

"By the way, Mr. and Mrs. Watson, I see from your papers that you hail from the same town in which I grew up and attended school."

Turning around, I asked, "I thought you were Australian by your accent?"

"Oh, yes, even though I'm a Canadian citizen now, I did live down-under for some years and acquired an Australian accent. I'm a bit of an actress, eh?"

"Where did you attend school in San Diego?" I asked.

"I attended La Jolla Junior-Senior High School and graduated in 1956. My father was a cardiologist in La Jolla."

I'm a bit of an actress stuck in my mind and as she talked I slowly realized that the Elizabeth Baker standing before me was once a tall, lanky blonde— a drama student of mine. I wouldn't have recognized her in a hundred years.

"I can't believe this!" I exclaimed. "I was the speech and drama teacher at La Jolla then and you're the Elizabeth Baker who was in my senior play."

There was a sudden realization that we had known each other at another time under different circumstances. We reminisced about the students and faculty; we laughed over trials and trauma of the senior play. It was like going home again...only for a few moments.

Then she admonished us, "Even though we've known each other previously, I shall conduct the hearing according to the law." Her voice was firm and serious. "I'll mail the hearing notices to Mr. Haddon and your neighbours immediately. See you in two weeks. Please don't tell anyone you've known me before. If anybody found out, it could affect your case." And we shook hands again.

14

WINNING THE BATTLE/
LOSING THE WAR

"What a coincidence knowing Elizabeth Baker. I can't believe she is the rentalsman," I said. "And here she was a student of mine." My statement was answered with silence. Maurie hurriedly drove the car to catch the ferry going to Salt Spring.

Oh, oh. When Maurie is quiet, that's not a good sign.

"What's the matter?" I asked.

"What's the matter?" he answered. "This is the second

time we've gotten into a mess with tenants and I'm tired of all the hassle. That's what's the matter. Christ! I've got enough legal problems at home with my practice...without all this in Canada."

"But there might be a chance to remove Haddon."

"Yah, by imposing on our neighbours to testify at a hearing. And how can you possibly ask your father to live up here for a year just so we can get our house back?"

We didn't speak for a long time.

I mustered my courage to ask a question—one troubling my mind for a long time. "Do you really like it up here?"

"I don't like it as much as you do, that's for sure. We've had fun with the kids and friends for a few years, I'll admit. But it's costing us money for this Canadian house. And remember, we have house payments to make on our new house in San Diego. After we get Haddon out, I'm ready to sell it. If we can't boot him out, then we'll sell it from beneath him."

It was my turn to be quiet. My mind churned along with the ferry as we departed from Swartz Bay.

We've had so many problems with the house. Maurie's right, it would be too much to ask Dad to stay up here for a year. But Haddon started all this. We've just got to get rid of him.

It upset me to return to the island with so much tension between us. We turned into our driveway and Haddon's car was gone. Maurie looked disgusted stepping over the mattress and walking by Haddon's junk. He marched downstairs like a determined general, composed a notice to pay rent, marched upstairs and tacked the notice to Haddon's door.

Relief came for the moment when Dad and Charlotte rolled up in Island Car. Being a good sport, Dad entertained her while we were in Victoria.

"What did you find out from the rentalsman?" Dad asked. We recapped our meeting describing the rentalsman's suggestions.

"Well, I got you both in this trouble with Haddon and I'd sure like to get you out. If I would use the house next year, would I have to be here all the time or could I go back and forth?"

"Don't even consider it, Bud," Maurie frowned. "It would be asking too much of you to stay up here for a year. We'll do our best to get that bastard out at the hearing with the evidence we have." Nothing more was said.

In our downstairs suite, Maurie, Charlotte and I lay in bed that night wondering if Haddon would return on the late ferry. After the ferry passed our house, we soon heard his car in driveway. There was one set of footsteps on the upstairs deck; Haddon was alone. The footsteps paused followed by heavy stomping downstairs to our door.

POUND, POUND, POUND. "Mr. Watson, I want to discuss this notice to pay rent," Haddon shouted.

Maurie sternly answered in the dark, "We've gone to bed, Mr. Haddon. I'll be happy to talk about the rent in the morning."

"But I want to talk about it NOW."

"Good night, Mr. Haddon."

Silence followed. Lighter footsteps tread upstairs and crossed the living room. Suddenly a thunderous pounding of a drum filled our lower suite and reverberated across the harbour. We sat up with a start and turned on the lights. We looked at each other and started to laugh over Haddon's antic.

"We gotta get the neighbours to witness this for the hearing—I'm sure they can hear the noise, " I said.

Maurie was laughing. "O.K. Let's do it. You girls sneak over to the Van Meels and I'll go get the Blacks. We'll meet in the driveway, but be quiet so he doesn't hear us."

We stealthily gathered the neighbours in the driveway—they stood in their night clothes listening to the steady drum beat. Haddon heard us talking in the dark and rushed outside. "You ass holes. What are you doing on my premises?"

Maurie shined his flashlight on Haddon's angry face. "You're disturbing the neighbourhood, Mr. Haddon. And we're not on your premises. Only the upstairs is yours, that is, if you pay the back rent."

"You're suddenly awake, Mr. Watson. You wouldn't talk to me a few minutes ago."

"I repeat. I'll talk to you in the morning about the notice to pay the rent, man to man. Right now you're acting childish. The neighbours are here to witness the noise you've been making as well as your rude behaviour."

"Ass holes," Haddon muttered as he walked back to the house. The harbour was quiet the rest of the night.

On the day of the hearing, the Blacks, Van Meels and Dad mustered with us in the driveway like a troop ready for battle. The mattress and the lounge chairs were gone. We waited for Elizabeth Baker who was to arrive on the afternoon ferry. When her car pulled into the driveway

and she emerged from it, she strode toward us with the
bearing of a queen. She spoke with authority, telling us
the procedure for the hearing. I gave her a knowing
look as our entourage followed her up to the back door.

Haddon met us, gushing with politeness. His girlfriend stood quietly by his side. "I appreciate your coming to the island for the hearing, Miss Baker. Please,
everyone come in and make yourselves comfortable."

"Thank you, Mr. Haddon," Elizabeth Baker
answered.

*What a change in character. He's so polite and
charming.*

None of us said a word as we seated ourselves
around the dining room table.

"We are gathered to hear testimony that will determine whether or not Mr. Haddon can continue his tenancy on this property owned by Mr. and Mrs. Maurice
Watson," Elizabeth Baker said. "I shall first hear
testimony from the Watsons and their neighbours and
then, Mr. Haddon, you can present your case. Let us
begin."

"I'd like to say that the mess in the carport and driveway are disgusting." Kas jumped right in. "The
Watsons have asked Mr. Haddon to clean it up several
times and he's ignored their requests. Besides, with this
dry weather we've been having, that junk is a fire
hazard."

"Please identify yourself when testifying, " Miss
Baker said.

"My name is Kas, that's spelled K-A-S and my last
name is Black."

"Thank you, please continue."

"You can put down on your record there, Miss Baker, that Archie Black, that's my name, thinks Haddon and his lady friend should not continue walking on the carport roof and dragging lounge furniture on it after the Watsons told them to stop. Those folks lounge up there in the sun and the legs on that furniture pokes holes in the roofing."

Miss Baker listened attentively. "Anyone else care to comment?"

"There are damages to our property unseen from the outside," Maurie said. "Haddon finally allowed me to inspect the inside of the house—I'm sure it's because he knew you were coming, Miss Baker. There is a bookcase with many shelves nailed to the wall in one of the bedrooms and we didn't give Mr. Haddon permission to do that. All these hanging pots we see over our heads in the living room have screw eyes in the beams to hold them up—there are a lot of holes in the beams now...and there are water spots on the carpet below. Just look at them."

Haddon had a stoic expression on his face.

"My name is Thea Van Meel and I just want to say that he was beating the drum in the middle of the night and disturbing the peace. He was giving the Watsons a bad time after they asked him to pay the rent. We came to this house after being awakened. He even called us ass holes."

"Yah, yah, I'm her husband, Jos, and I say that the way they lie around on the mattress in the driveway with their bare-assed butts, that they're the ass-holes."

Elizabeth Baker raised her eyebrows and requested, "Let's watch our language, Mr. Van Meel." Then she added, "I didn't see the mattress there today."

"No," Jos answered, "he took it away because you were comin'."

My mind drifted as the hearing continued. The door to the upstairs deck was open letting in the fresh air and sunshine, allowing freedom to blow in, freedom from the problems inside the room. I wanted our house back, the way it was, not with tangled hanging plants and ugly tenants inside, without conflict.

Miss Baker looked at me. "Mrs. Watson, do you care to say anything?"

Her question brought me back to reality. "Yes, I do. As you can see, he has upset our neighbours and he's really upset us. He's a very difficult man. He hasn't done what we asked, like clean up the mess outside and take the lounge chairs off the roof...and he hasn't paid the rent for two months. He agreed to move out August 1 when my father rented to him last November...and here it is, near the end of August and he hasn't moved. He's very pushy. Last spring he wrote us a letter asking to move the carport away from the house to make a patio for sunning and to cut a window at the end of the living room for more light. We refused to do that. We didn't want to spend the money. And he became angry about it."

"I see." Miss Baker wrote notes. "Any other comments?" There was silence. "Now it's your turn, Mr. Haddon."

Haddon began his response with the sincerity of an angel. "Miss Baker, these people don't understand that I was merely trying to improve the property for Mr. and Mrs. Watson. I have enjoyed the view and the sunshine here. Why should I do anything detrimental to the property?"

"Mr. Haddon, your wanting to improve the property is irrelevant because, you see, it's not your property," Elizabeth Baker quickly pointed out.

Haddon continued his testimony. "The things of which they complain were done innocently and I can certainly rectify anything. I've done no major damage and I see no legal cause to terminate my tenancy."

This guy's been around. He's right and knows we have a weak case.

Dad, sensing the strength of Haddon's argument, blurted out, "Miss Baker, excuse me. My name is Bud Whiteman. I'm Mrs. Watson's father. I think I'd like to stay in this house during the coming year. What must I do?"

Maurie frowned, took off his glasses and rubbed his eyes—his habit when dealing with difficult problems.

Haddon glared at my father, "You interrupted me, Mr. Whiteman, while I was explaining my position."

Miss Baker put up her hand as if stopping traffic. "Please wait, Mr. Haddon. It's true Mr. Whiteman interrupted you. But I must ask him a few questions. His request may change the situation. Mr. Whiteman, how much time would you plan to be on the island?"

"You see, I'm widowed and I'd like a change," Dad said. " So, perhaps, I'd be here about three-quarters of the year. I would travel back to my condo in Southern California periodically."

"Mr. Whiteman, when would you want to start using the property?"

"Well, I'll have to go home to make some arrangements, but I'd like to start in October."

I can't believe what I'm hearing. Dad is trying to save us again.

Elizabeth Baker shuffled through her papers for a moment, paused and said, "If that's the case, then according to the landlord-tenant laws of British Columbia, the landlord's need to use the property for his family are grounds for termination of tenancy. Also failure to pay rent is cause for termination. Therefore, Mr. Haddon, there's no need for further testimony. I'll give you until September 30 to vacate this property. That gives you a little over a month to look for new quarters. Mr. Whiteman, you can take occupancy on October 1. Mr. and Mrs. Watson, I'll send you and Mr. Haddon all the paper work necessary for the termination."

Haddon looked like a whipped dog.

An air of relief swept over the room. Dad gave me a big smile; then I saw Maurie's dour expression. Ambivalent feelings hit me.

"Is there any further discussion?" Miss Baker asked, looking around the room. There was a long pause. I watched Maurie, knowing he objected to the commitment Dad was about to make, but he kept silent.

"Then this hearing is closed," Miss Baker declared. "Now, I must catch the next ferry back to Victoria. Mr. Haddon, would you and your friend please step outside for a private word."

With Haddon gone, everyone shook Dad's hands and patted him on the back...except Maurie.

Miss Baker returned to the living room. "Thank you everyone for coming. I think the problem is resolved. Mr. Haddon and his friend have left for awhile. Mr. and Mrs. Watson, would you please accompany me to my car?"

We strolled slowly to Miss Baker's car. "I think you should try to get Haddon to leave voluntarily before

October 1," Elizabeth Baker quietly said. "It would be preferable to my doing all the legal procedures."

"How can we do that?" Maurie asked, then thought for a moment. "The only way I can think of is to maybe pay him the August rent to get him out of here by September 1."

"Good idea. Try it and see what happens. Then call me at the office." Miss Baker replied.

We thanked her as she got into her car. She shot a look at me. "How was my performance?"

I quietly smiled. "You played your role beautifully."

The next day Maurie went upstairs to offer Haddon the August rent provided he move off the premises with all his belongings by September 1. Haddon accepted the offer. He and his girlfriend scurried around for the next few days packing up their belongings. They left promising to return to clean up the carport, but they never came back. Cyril saw Haddon once or twice in the village after that. Maurie contacted Elizabeth Baker about our success in removing Haddon after which time she closed the case.

Dad tried to atone for his bad choice of a tenant by living in the island house periodically during the year. Again, he cleaned up a second mess left behind by troublesome tenants. After that year, he only returned to the island one more time for soon he would meet Catherine while doing volunteer work in an Orange County hospital.   His loneliness and melancholy gradually faded away in her presence. Happy days returned to my father when they married.

Winning the battle of removing Haddon brought no rental income for a year. When we could legally rent again, Maurie said, "I don't want to go to the island next summer...I'm ready to sell the house."

15

HOUSE FOR SALE

Like manna from heaven, Dennis and Carol Scott, our former tenants, heard about our vacant house and wanted to rent it again. They sold their new home and used the profits to start a small clothing store in the village. Carolee's and Michael's was the name of the shop; Dennis continued working at the Trading Post grocery store.

But Maurie wasn't keen on the idea.

"Maurie, please consider renting the house to the Scotts," I appealed to him. "We know they're reliable people. They'll take good care of the place."

"Look, after all the problems with Haddon, I want to sell the damn thing," he answered. "We've had two tenants who were disasters...that house is costing us money."

"I know, I know." I felt heartsick, wanting so much to change his mind. I struggled with what to say next. "...ah, how about stepping back from the house for awhile..."

"What do you mean?"

"You said you didn't want to go back up there. Well, let's rent the house to the Scotts for as long as they want it...and accrue a little money in our Canadian bank account...try to catch up with our debts. Then, when they move out, decide what we'll do with the house."

"I've already decided what we'll do with the house," he shot back angrily.

The Scotts said they wanted to rent over the winter.

"Please, Maurie, we won't be bothered with the house for awhile. Please hold off selling. What do we have to lose?"

To my great relief, Maurie reluctantly consented to renting.

During that time, America was hit by recession; there was a 12% inflation rate. Maurie's law firm changed from a partnership to a corporation requiring payment of taxes for two fiscal years within one year. Our son Scott was enrolled in a community college and about to transfer to university; we were anticipating college costs for Charlotte. I returned to full-time teaching, just to help pay the taxes. Then, Maurie submitted his name for a Federal judgeship, an appointment that would mean more of a drop in income. For extra money, I took an additional part-time teaching job at a community college. Teaching night and day and raising two kids was not easy.

Good people came through in the wake of misfortune for a second time. The Scotts maintained the house as if it were their own. Dennis called Maurie: "The outside of your house really needs painting. If you're willing to pay for the paint, I'll paint it for you." Instead of troubles, our island house received care and a fresh coat of green paint.

Next door, tragedy struck the Van Meels. It happened on a Thursday before a long holiday. Jos and Thea had packed their boat in anticipation of a long cruise over the Canada Day weekend. Jos was planning to take a break from building a house located on some acreage with a farmhouse and a large barn. On that Thursday, he crawled up a long ladder to the hayloft in the barn to check on construction material stored there. Suddenly he lost his balance at the top of the ladder and fell crashing to the floor, hitting his head on a band saw.

Just then, a physician on his holiday was cycling by, saw Jos staggering in front of the barn bleeding profusely from his ear and offered some assistance. The foreman on the job called for an ambulance from Lady Minto Hospital; then he called Thea and her daughter Barbara to meet Jos at the hospital. When they arrived, Jos was thrashing about and vomiting. His condition became traumatic, so the hospital ordered a helicopter to fly him to Royal Jubilee Hospital in Victoria.

Thea told us later what happened in Victoria:

"We followed Jos to Victoria by taking the ferry. Oh, it seemed so slow. Since it was a holiday weekend there were lots of tourists—the traffic was terrible. And there was no place to stay overnight. We finally found a motel on Dallas Road and insisted that the manager wire a telephone in our room in case the hospital wanted to call us. Of course, we didn't sleep much.

"Jos was in intensive care for a few days because the swelling from his head injury wouldn't go away. Then, he improved a little and was sitting up in bed...even ate a hamburger. One day I brought him some clam chowder in a thermo flask. I also peeled a peach for him. He seemed to enjoy everything.

"Jos was not one to complain easily, so when he said, 'I have a terrible headache,' he must have had a fierce pain.

"'I wish I could have the headache for you,' I told him.

"He took my hand and kissed all my fingers. That was the last time I saw Jos alive in the hospital. His condition worsened and he was put on life support. A day later he had a cat scan and was pronounced brain dead...that's when the life support was disconnected."

Such difficult times for Thea after Jos' death. Her daughter Barbara came to live with her on the island and Thea clung to her like a lifeline.

An island can be a lonely place.

I dreaded the day when the Scotts gave notice they were moving into their own home. The stalling was over. The day of reckoning at hand. Maurie had remained firm in wanting to sell the house.

"I've made reservations for one-way tickets for us and the kids to fly up to Canada this summer," he said. "Then we'll drive Island Car home with anything we want to keep after we clean up the house and put it on the market."

Defeated in my efforts to change his mind, there was nothing more I could say. I knew that I must support him in what he wanted to do. I knew if he was appointed to the bench, we couldn't afford the island house.

It was a bittersweet vacation. The kids caught rock cod and picked blackberries knowing it would be their last time; they tenderly watered the two young trees they had planted near the back porch. Our island friends, especially Carrie Louise and Cyril, were crestfallen that we were selling our house. Carrie looked so solemn, sometimes finding it difficult to speak to us. Kas, in her blunt way, said, "We don't want you to go. You're fools to sell because the value of property on the island will increase."

We staged a yard sale in our driveway. I watched our furniture and belongings loaded into cars and vans. It was as if a part of me was taken away. The brown couch from the Victoria Goodwill was toted off—it represented victory over one tenant and defeat by another. A gas station took our boat to sell on consignment. We left it parked on the garage lot next to the Fulford-Ganges Road.

Closing the house was painful. When Maurie nailed a *For Sale* sign on the railing, I felt like the nails were piercing my heart. When we stopped by the

Cunninghams to say our last goodbye before catching the ferry, Carrie Louise's eyes were on the brink of tears. My throat tightened up as we stood on the deck of the *Queen of Nanaimo* leaving Long Harbour.

Take a good look. I told myself. *Keep the tears back. This is the last time you'll see the house.*

Maurie stood by my side. I bravely watched our passing house nestled among the trees, its cathedral windows shimmering in the afternoon sun. The ferry steamed out of the harbour. I turned away and couldn't look back.

"I'm proud of you," Maurie said, "I know this isn't easy."

Tsawwassen terminal came into view three hours later and we headed for San Diego in Island Car, loaded with mementos. Familiar towns whizzed by. It seemed like an endless trip through long stretches of silence.

The recession remained, not only in America, but also in Canada. We received one offer to buy the house. In retrospect, it was a substantial offer for those economic times, but Maurie turned it down, reasoning that our house was worth more. He was wrong. There were no more offers.

Our taxes were paid but I continued to teach part-time in the community college. The usual politics of gender, color, political party and the "old boy network" had kept Maurie from his desired appointment to the bench. It was waste of judicial ability and temperament.

In the winter of 1983, another ladder accident. Cyril fell while climbing up to his roof. He re-injured his knee which prohibited him from caring for our property. During Easter vacation, I flew to Canada with my friend Hortensia Emery to spur the realtor on to sell our house...and to find someone to manage it. Cyril and Carrie Louise met us at Victoria Airport.

"Honey, we're so glad to see ya'll back," Carrie Louise said, giving me a long hug. "You gotta stay with us cause there's not a stick of furniture in your place. Poor Cyril hasn't been able to do a thing for you."

"I'm sorry, Cyril, that you had an accident," I said. "Here, let me give you a great big kiss."

The little man beamed. "Welcome back. We must have a drink when we get home." Cyril limped badly as he talked. "By the way, you're welcome to use our extra car while you're on the island."

It felt so good to be on the Fulford ferry again, heading for Salt Spring. The island in the spring rains looked green and lush with dogwood and azaleas in bloom along the way. Newly-born lambs were grazing. The air was fresh and pure. A huge sense of release rose within me, a calm, a relief I hadn't felt for two years.

Hortensia and I drove to our house the next day for an inspection. Green weeds were knee deep. Piles of arbutus leaves covered the decks. The cobwebs were back, laced between the eaves. One of the little balsam firs I had planted with the kids died; one tree, thank goodness, had survived. It was a depressing sight for I remembered how beautiful our house looked before.

No wonder this place hasn't sold. It looks awful. We've got to do something about it. The house just can't sit here.

Soon, the realtor came to the house and I took him inside.

"Property values are in a slump, Mrs. Watson," the realtor said. "Very little is being sold on the island now. I've shown your property, but it's the recession, eh? People simply don't have the money. You might consider lowering the price...or taking it off the market for awhile."

"Yes, I know it hasn't been a good time to sell, but it's been over two years since we listed it. My husband really wants to get rid of it. Let me talk to him about lowering the price...maybe taking it off the market. I'll get back to you."

Inwardly I yearned to be in the house again, to fix it up, to furnish it, to make it comfortable.

I called Maurie long-distance from the Cunninghams. "The realtor told me houses aren't selling up here because of the recession. Everything's in the doldrums. Do you want to reduce the price?"

There was silence at the end of the line. Then a firm "no" hit my ear.

"How about taking if off the market...and..." I held my breath as I delicately suggested..."renting the upstairs again...unfurnished?"

A long pause, then came the answer. "There's not much choice, is there?" Then a sigh. "If we can't sell it, we might as well rent it and get *some* money from it."

What beautiful words to my ears! Here was a slight chance to keep the house.

"Is it O.K. to cancel the listing with the realtor?" I tried to keep my voice from sounding too excited.

"Yes," Maurie answered. "Christ, I'm going to have to fill out those complicated income tax forms again."

"How about the downstairs suite?"

"What about it?"

"Well..." using a coquettish voice, "maybe, while I'm up here, I can find some used furniture for the downstairs. Then we could use it again while we're renting the upstairs."

"Jacque, I know what you're up to," he sighed. I could feel him giving in. "Go ahead and see what you can find."

16

TURNING OF THE TIDE

I was ecstatic. I yelled to Carrie Louise, "Carrie, Maurie said that I can take the house off the market and rent it!"

Carrie Louise rushed over to me and we hugged each other. "Oh, honey, I'm so glad he'll let you do that."

"It's a chance to keep the house...and Maurie said I can look for some used furniture for the downstairs suite too."

"That's wonderful." Carrie's face radiated with joy. "You'll be back on the island in no time."

I was so excited that I called our neighbours to tell them the good news. "I knew you'd smarten up, " Kas replied, " I tell you, that house is a good investment."

"I'm happy you're coming back," Thea said. "You're haven't been in your house for such a long time. Oh, it's looked so dark next door."

"It's looked so dark..." Thea's words hit me, like lightening strikes. The days did look dark; in fact they seemed black. Our lack of money, the judgeship not coming through, the house not selling and not knowing what would happen— all were disheartening. My dreams had become my nightmares. Yet the negative events, beyond my control, ironically met my unanswered prayers. Good luck waited in the bad. Each problem, each frustration had been pointing all the time toward keeping the house on Long Harbour. It was still ours! A rush of excitement swept over me. Happiness welled within my heart. *It's a second chance.*

I couldn't wait for the Wednesday edition of the *Driftwood*. When it came out, I combed the advertisements for garage sales. One listing caught my eye:

> Garage Sale on Beddis Road. Chesterfield, tables, rocking chair, appliances, knick-knacks. Saturday and Sunday. Call 537-9727.

I took Hortensia and Carrie Louise on a rainy afternoon down an endless road that ran parallel with Ganges Harbour in search of used furniture. There, in an islander's garage, a brown rocking chair, somewhat worn on the arms, looked like it belonged in our house.

I purchased it for \$15. I was tickled with the bargain—the old rocking chair represented a new beginning, the first step toward furnishing the house again.

A couple days later I borrowed a station wagon with the idea of stopping at the Victoria Goodwill after I took Hortensia to tea at the Empress Hotel. Good fortune smiled again. A comfortable sofa bed recovered in gold tweed with a reconditioned, sanitized mattress for \$150 had just been placed on the shop floor. "Sold!" I said. With my second purchase snug in the back of the wagon, I whistled all the way back to the island. *Now, we have something to sit on and to sleep on when we come up next summer. I am soooooooooooooo happy!*

"Dicey" is a word often used by Canadians...and the British. It's a colourful word meaning iffy, uncertain, provisional. Maurie and I returned to the island in August of 1986 and lived in the downstairs suite for about a month—and it was "dicey."

Maurie obviously didn't share my jubilant feelings of returning. I happily cleaned and scrubbed the house to the music lilting from the radio. By contrast, he was quiet—a signal that he wasn't keen about being there. Sometimes, during a meal, he didn't say a word. He attacked the weeds in the yard with a vengeance, so much so, that he burnt out the weedeater.

One night, after dinner in our downstairs suite was finished, we walked outside on the lower deck to watch the lingering sunset. I put my head on his shoulder and

164   **JACQUELINE WATSON**

softly asked, "How do you feel about being up here again?"

There was a pause. "I feel like a midget," he answered.

"What do you mean you feel like a midget—you're six feet, four?"

"I feel like a midget in a crowded elevator—I don't know which way to turn."

I laughed and nudged him, "Well, at least you haven't lost your sense of humour."

"I'm resigned to the situation," he sighed. "I just hope we get some good tenants and some money coming in."

I slipped my arms around his waist and kissed him on the cheek. "We will," I whispered. I felt his arms around my shoulders. There was light kiss on my brow. He guided me back into the seclusion of our downstairs suite.

Migs called to welcome us. "Wes and I are delighted to have you back on the island, albeit in your downstairs suite. How about coming over for dinner Saturday night...in our new home on Maracaibo?" Migs and Wes had sold the home on Southey Point and had built a Schubart-designed cedar house overlooking Long Harbour and the ferry terminal.

"Yes, we'd love to," I replied. "How's Maracaibo coming along?"

"You'll be pleasantly surprised," Migs said. "Since the Bare Lands Strata Title Act passed in '76,

Maracaibo has developed 71 strata title lots. And...did you know I sold Toad Hall to the Beckmanns?"

"That's wonderful."

"They were perfect people to buy our summer cottage. They'll be coming Saturday night too."

"We'll look forward to seeing them," I said. "By the way, we're going to have our Mexican party this summer. You and the Beckmanns are invited."

"How are you going to manage that in you downstairs suite?"

"We're going to have it at the Cunninghams."

"I am so glad. We've missed your taco parties."

Carrie Louise was a wonderful help to me in furnishing the downstairs suite. We traveled from Victoria to Duncan (both on Vancouver Island) in search of furnishings. While we went on our shopping excursions, Maurie stayed on the island doing repairs, splitting wood and working in the yard.

"Maurie, we found some treasures in a second-hand store in Duncan today," I said as Carrie and I carried in a formica kitchen table, then two vinyl chairs. "The set cost a 100 bucks...and it's in excellent condition."

"Your wife has a real eye for a bargain," Carrie Louise chuckled.

A slight smile from Maurie. "I'll start calling her the thrift shop queen." His solemn mood seemed to be changing. He became amused over my earnest search for bargains. "Maybe I'll go with you on your next treasure hunt." he said.

"It's fun. I've never shopped in second-hand stores or thrift shops before coming to Canada," I said. "This ceramic lamp for $5 was a steal." Out of a box I showed him a salad bowl for $1, two candlesticks for 50 cents each, kitchen glasses a $1 each and flatware for 50 cents a piece. "We'll get this place furnished in no time. Huh, Carrie Louise."

Carrie winked back at me. "We shore will, honey."

For a second time I ordered drapes from Simpson-Sears for both levels. I found inexpensive rubber-backed nylon carpeting at a discount store in Victoria and hired an islander to lay the carpeting upstairs and down. We repainted the upstairs bathrooms, changed light fixtures, washed curtains, and added double-paned windows to conserve heat. Finally, the house was clean, the yard tidy, and the upstairs ready to rent.

A young Australian and his wife, Bryan and Ann Lister, rented our house. He was a casual engineer (casual means part-time in Canada) with the B.C. Ferries. Handsome, young and cocky, he spoke with a delightful Aussie accent. Ann Lister, who hailed from Nova Scotia, was soft-spoken, attractive and feminine.

At that time, Dennis Scott managed the property, however Bryan took care of our house like it was his own. The yard was neatly trimmed. With our permission he installed a fireplace insert to economize on heating costs and built closet shelves. The steady income and excellent maintenance improved Maurie's attitude; the house was no longer a burden.

It was a pleasure to fly up to Canada in 1987 and stay in the downstairs suite for a few days. The Listers made owning the house easier. They transformed the upstairs into a decorator's delight. Antique furniture, ladened with doilies, graced the living room and bedroom. Bowls of dried petals filled the air with a pleasant aroma. Potted plants accented the furniture and enhanced the natural greenery outside. I admired Ann's flair for decorating.

We trusted being on the island. It was like going home again, seeing our island friends and being unencumbered by problems. Maurie and I eagerly anticipated a two-week cruise on a chartered boat to Desolation Sound with San Diego friends, Jim and Joan Reynolds. Being seasoned sailors, Jim was the skipper and Joan the chief galley cook. Exploring Desolation Sound and Princess Louisa Inlet under their guidance wetted out appetites to return someday.

That summer, there was an air of expectancy in our house for the Listers were to have their first baby. A charming baby's crib stood at the foot of their bed. Bryan happily built what he called "a mother-in-law" bed for Ann's mother who was coming from Nova Scotia. It pleased me to know there would soon be a baby in our house.

It contrasted with our own family situation: my dad was dying. Catherine had struggled for nearly a year caring for him. Although cancer was slowly consuming him, Maurie and I promised to have an afternoon 80th birthday celebration in mid-August for him and his New York cousin who would be 80 and my aunt (his sister) who would be 85. I had resolved, after my mother's death, to do whatever I could for my father when he needed me, especially when his time came. We left the island, after a delightful cruise, to prepare for the party.

Dad exemplified the strength of the human spirit; he willed himself to live for the party. As debilitating as his cancer was, he eagerly looked forward to the birthday party when his family clan and friends would gather together.

However, on the morning of the party, Catherine said, "Bud's not feeling too well. I wonder if he's strong enough leave the condo in his wheelchair and go to the party."

"Well, Catherine, the party is in the recreation room—nearby," I answered. "Let's see how he is this afternoon."

Cousins reunited for the first time in years, standing with arms around each other, bearing big smiles for photographs. Three cakes stood in a row decorated with sugar roses and birthday wishes. Enlarged photographs, posted around the room, showed images of Dad, my aunt and the New York cousin as babies, children and shining youths. My aunt and her cousin carried the day greeting, embracing and visiting with guests.

Someone asked me, "Where's Bud?"

"He's not feeling good today," I answered. Then I winced inwardly. *He's got to come to the party. He's looked forward to this day for so long,*

I asked Maurie and Scott to go to Dad's condo with me. Catherine and her family were with him. "Catherine, why don't you all go to the party and we'll stay with Dad for awhile."

"Promise to be careful with Bud," Catherine said as she reluctantly left.

When we were alone with Dad, he asked, "How's the party going?"

"It's going fine," I answered. "We just wish you were there."

"Well, what's holding me back? Catherine's gone. She thought I shouldn't go to the party. Get me dressed and I'll get over there."

"That's the ol' spirit, Dad." The three of us struggled to dress him, I put his black Greek hat on his bare head and we rolled him in his wheelchair to the party.

It was a bittersweet moment when Dad entered the room. There were handshakes, there were tears, there were hugs, there were whispered comments among the crowd. His facial expression was sober as he gazed into each face, knowing it would be his last time. The traditions of a birthday party took place—candles lit, a birthday song and toasts. Dad attended his party for 30 minutes, then became too weak to stay. From that point on, he gave in to the cancer, his body gradually wound down and he died six days later. I had helped him fulfill his wish; my heart felt no remorse after his death.

The days of fall were filled with settling Dad's affairs. Thea called during this time to announce that the Listers' baby was born. "Such a darling baby girl. Her name is Amy." Thea said. "Since Bryan is gone so much...working on the ferries, I've gotten to know Ann a little better."

"I'm glad you've become close neighbours," I answered.

"Yes, we often have coffee together. She's very lonely you know, feels isolated. He loves the island, but she doesn't like it at all."

That's just the opposite of Maurie and me. People either love the island or they're very unhappy there.

"I feel sorry for her," Thea continued, "so I run errands for her and help with the baby."

"That's good for both of you."

Another phone call from Thea in the middle of winter. "Something terrible has happened to your tenants!"

"What is it, Thea? What's happened?" I was fearful something had happened to them in the house.

"The other night Ann came rushing over to my house carrying her baby and it was screaming."

"What was the matter with the baby?" I asked.

"I didn't know at first. Then Ann frantically said. 'I was holding Amy under my arm, she slipped through and fell on her head on the kitchen floor. She's been screaming ever since.'"

"I took Amy in my arms and she cried all the time," Thea said, "and she didn't look so good, kinda pale."

"'Thea, I can't quiet her. Amy just vomited. I'm scared. I don't know what to do.'"

"Let's take her in my car to emergency at Lady Minto Hospital, right away,' I told Ann."

"What happened then?" I asked.

"The doctor on duty examined Amy and immediately ordered a helicopter to fly them to Vancouver. I returned to your house, gathered up the baby and mother's belongings and caught a ferry to Tsawwassen by way of Fulford."

"Thea, how wonderful of you to do that," I said.

"When I arrived at the hospital in Vancouver, Ann met me and was so upset. 'Amy is in the trauma unit,' she said, 'and has a concussion. They want to keep her there for surveillance. Oh, Thea, it's all my fault.'"

"I tried to comfort her," Thea said, "but she was beside herself."

From that point on, behind the closed doors of our house, a marriage mysteriously disintegrated. Thea kept us informed about the turn of events.

"Amy continues to have problems. The concussion has had lasting effects." Then Thea sighed, "Poor Bryan is working off-island as far north as the Queen Charlotte Islands and isn't able to be with Ann and the baby very much."

"I feel so sorry for them, Thea," I said. "I wish I could do something for them."

"I'm helping as much as I can, but Ann is so lonely..."

In the spring of 1988 we received notice from the Listers that they were vacating our house. I called Thea immediately, "What's happened with the Listers? They've given notice they're leaving."

"They've separated," Thea answered. "It's a pity. Ann has taken the baby and gone back to Nova Scotia to be with her mother."

"Where's Bryan?" I asked.

"Bryan is still on the island, working for the ferries."

I winced and thought life is ironic...so unpredictable. The Listers were desirable tenants, conscientious in their care of our house, a sharp contrast to the undesirables we couldn't get rid of in the past. We wanted them to stay, yet they were leaving.

Their departure forced us to think about the house again. I'll never forget the evening in San Diego when Maurie and I were discussing what to do.

"You know, Jacque, our finances are in better shape since I formed the corporation." Maurie was thinking out loud.

"Good," I answered.

"We're just about off the hook financially with the kids' college."

"Thank goodness," I replied.

"There's been steady rental money from the Listers."

"Yes," I wondered what he was leading to.

"And we've owned the house for fifteen years. The mortgage on the house is nearly paid."

"Yeah, so, what are you thinking?"

Maurie smiled, gave me a long look, then said, "Why don't we pay off the balance... and not be hassled with renting the house anymore?"

It took me a moment to understand what he just said. "Oh, Maurie Watson, I can't believe it! You mean have the whole house for ourselves?"

"Yes, have the whole house for ourselves."

I was so excited. I threw my arms around him and gave him a big kiss. My mind was awhirl, "I've got a brainstorm."

"Geez, here we go again. What is it this time?" Maurie asked.

"Why don't we take the furniture from Dad's condo and put it upstairs in the Canadian house?"

"Oh, Jacque, not another 1,400 mile trip pulling a trailer full of used furniture!"

"Yes, think of the money we'd save. Dad would be so pleased to have his furniture on Salt Spring."

Such a pilgrimage that summer of 1988. Maurie drove our car pulling a U-Haul trailer loaded with my parents' furniture. We still had Island Car. Charlotte drove it to college, but she relinquished it for its return to Salt Spring. I drove it north: steadily rolling through the flat fields of the San Joaquin Valley; ascending the mountains cradling Lake Shasta; weaving through the congested traffic of Portland and Seattle; following log trucks, so close, I smelled the aroma of saw dust; boarding the Long Harbour ferry with its welcoming sounds of clang and clatter; arriving on the island, green and quiet.

Unloading the familiar furniture, carefully carrying each piece into the house, and finding its special place brought nostalgia to my heart. My parents' lives were over, their chapters finished; only memories remained. Yet their old furniture fit perfectly in the bedrooms, along walls, upstairs and down, comforting to see, like their pieces had become part of our story.

The Listers left the house in good order except for a sprinkling of burnt spots on the carpeting underneath the fireplace. We purchased a fireproof area rug to cover the damage and sent the bill to Bryan. No reply from him. Then, one Saturday, we accidentally met him at the Farmers' Market. It was an awkward meeting— we were surprised to see him, he was embarrassed to see us. His emotions were bottled and constricted behind his handsome face; the cockiness gone. A short conversation. He hesitantly agreed to send us a check for the rug, then dejectedly walked on.

Bryan was our last full-time tenant.

17
NOTICEABLE CHANGES

B y 1988 we had not enjoyed the whole house for five years. During that time, I missed not making our yearly summer pilgrimage. I missed the excitement of preparing to go to the island, the anticipation of having house guests, the packing, the planning ahead for our Mexican party. I missed the change of scenery, the change of faces, the change of pace, the solitude of the forest and the quiet of the harbour. I missed Mrs. Wiedswang's cooking!

My instinct to go north had been conditioned over the years. Just as a migratory bird heads north in the spring, I too had an inner urge to head toward the island. Salt Spring was a wonderful escape hatch from my daily stresses and routines; life was easier up there. I was not aware of my connectedness to the island until I was separated from it.

Maurie's sentiments were not the same as mine. I knew in my heart they never would be. He felt relieved from the burdens of the house during our absence. Out of sight, out of mind. He enjoyed the freedom of traveling to other places for vacation and not going to the island every summer; he believed the variety of travel was broadening for our children. Maurie was a good sport about keeping the house. However, deep down, from his viewpoint, the Beachcomber's prophecy had come true—he was "stuck" on the island. An underlying difference of feeling remained between us—subtle, but ever present.

Those few years brought noticeable changes. Along Marina Crescent Drive, the Garry oaks, arbutus, cedars and pines were thinned out, replaced by houses. Next door, the attractive house designed by Hank Schubart stood unobtrusively in the trees; Netboy was still the owner. The hill above us sprouted homes. A sprinkling of small docks lined our side of Long Harbour. Freshly-built houses bordered Welbury Bay and Scott Point Drive; few vacant lots remained.

Typical of new houses built at that time was one on the south side of Scott Point—owned by two newcomers, friends of ours from San Diego, Harry and Barbara French. The Frenches, retired from the restaurant business, were smitten by the beauty of Salt Spring Island while on a fishing trip to April Point. They bought a scenic lot with a southwest vista of ferries crossing in the distance; Matthew Schubart, Hank Schubart's son, designed their two-story home. In 1987 they shipped their boat to Ganges Marina, migrated north and became landed immigrants. The Frenches were one small part of the population growth slowly infiltrating Salt Spring Island in the late '80s.

Across Long Harbour on Maracaibo, scattered subtly among the trees, were outlines of new construction, houses taking form within the rules of Maracaibo's building covenant. Canadians from Vancouver, Edmonton, Saskatoon and Toronto were slowly discovering Maracaibo, joining the association and building their retirement homes. At night, house lights twinkled where it had been dark before.

We took a Sunday drive in Island Car to visit the Beckmanns at Toad Hall. Paul and Elizabeth and their family fit comfortably into the Russell cottage like an old shoe. Beyond the Beckmann's driveway, a paved road led to Maracaibo building sites strung along a road to the end of Nose Point. Close by, in the core area, we were surprised to see so many changes: families sunbathing on the lawn next to the pond, a wooden gazebo standing center stage in the core area, Charles Moat's old house converted to a clubhouse, wind-surfers skimming across the end of Long Harbour, kayaks replacing canoes on the beach, a long dock lined with pleasure boats stretching parallel to the shore.

Jack Russell's vision for Maracaibo has come true. He may be gone from this earth, but his blueprint remains.

In Ganges, during the last two years of the sewer stink, 1984-86, building had come to almost a standstill. The village had fallen behind in providing shopping, goods and services to 7,000 or so islanders. Ganges had a lot of catching up to do; money was going off-island.

Then, with the sewer completion, a boom hit Ganges Village.

"You'll be surprised at all the changes when you go into Ganges," Cyril told us. "It's getting to be an attractive little spot with lots of amenities."

One Saturday morning we climbed in Island Car to see for ourselves, knowing full well the village would be busy with Farmers' Market. However, when we were forced to join a car line slowly creeping into town, we were shocked. Parking was impossible; the core area and side roads were overflowing with parked cars. Tourists marched in droves into the village.

"Look at all the people milling around Farmers' Market," I said. "The market has grown like topsy. It looks like a flea market instead of a Farmers' Market."

Stalls and umbrellas covered the length of Centennial Park and spilled around to the sides. Some sellers were clean and scrubbed while others looked like they crawled out of the woods. They displayed birdhouses, pottery, earrings, pins, cards, knick-knacks of all kinds. Levis, cushions, towels, T-shirts, purses— piled high—were obviously not island products. Mixed aromas from food stands, serving everything from Mexican food to designer coffees, wafted through the air. A large truck, loaded with produce, displayed a sign, "Okanagan Produce." Okanagan valley was a fruit and produce farming area east of Vancouver. A few remnants of the old Farmers' Market, such as flowers, baked goods and vegetables, remained, but they were overshadowed by the commercialism of off-island traders.

We strolled to Grace Point where the wooded penin- sula once stood opposite Mouat's. The trees and the storage tanks had disappeared and in their place rose two-story wooden townhouses—gray, beige and under- stated, snuggled into the rocks. The commercial proper- ty adjacent to Grace Point was replaced by Grace Point Square, a shopping complex with similar architecture— reminiscent of shops in Canon Beach, Oregon or Nantucket.

The metamorphosis of Ganges village was slowly taking place. The square bland storefront buildings located on the west side of Fulford-Ganges Road were torn down. In their place, Creekhouse, a cluster of fash- ionable shops, straddled the creek which flowed from above Ganges into the harbour. The gray clapboard was a two-story, gabled structure. Wooden decking in front of Creekhouse served as a bridge and a boardwalk over the creek. Segments of a boardwalk were built at water's edge near Centennial Park and on the northeast side of Ganges Harbour. Across the street from

Creekhouse, a long narrow building called Gasoline Alley stretched to the harbour; it housed small shops and a restaurant. I was particularly pleased to find a spiffy, new laundromat in the building.

Driving up Lower Ganges Road, which had been bordered by rolling hills with clusters of trees, skeletal frames of condominiums were rising in tidy rows overlooking the harbour; they reminded us of a California subdivision. A strip development of small buildings plus the island's first supermarket lay north along Lower Ganges Road.

I sat on our deck that evening, listening to the quiet of Long Harbour. Just as it had done for thousands of years, the sun set in a deep red glow. The seagulls still called out. The fresh, night air filled my lungs. The smooth tide calmly flowed into the harbour. I reflected upon the changes we had seen.

I went inside where Maurie was reading and settled into a book of my own. Faintly, noises came from outside—boat noises. I looked through the windows and there in the shadows of the early night was a long, metal boat moving slowly along the Maracaibo shore. A spotlight beamed upon a net dragging from behind.

"Look at that boat," I said. "What's it doing over there?"

Maurie went out on the deck to get a better look. He sighed, "It's a herring boat. I've seen them before coming into Long Harbour and setting nets for herring. The only trouble is, every living thing is caught too."

"That's terrible. What will happen to the fish that feed on them?"

"They probably won't come up the harbour anymore."

I became angry when I thought of the shimmering herring swirling in schools just below the surface of the water. How beautifully iridescent they looked. Now they would be gone. I remembered the happy day when Tom Toynbee caught a beautiful salmon in Long Harbour—it had been lured by the herring.

I thought about the crabbers on Long Harbour—commercial crabbing boats that dropped their countless steel wire traps in the harbour, then returned after a few days to pull them up full of Dungeness crab. I realized there were no controls—no protection for the sea life; it was gradually being scraped away before our eyes. *Even here, we can't avoid being affected by change.*

"Welcome back to the island." It was Loes' cheery voice on the phone. "I've missed you."

"Thank you, Loes," I said. "It's so nice to be back. To be able to live in the whole house again."

"That's a good thing you didn't sell it, eh? How's Maurie?"

"He's fine. And Gerry?"

"He's getting old, you know. Can't do as much, but he manages."

"Are you still going on trips?"

"Sure. I just came back from voooonderful trip to Ecuador with my daughter Joy. Ve vent to the Galapagos on a small ship to see all the animals. You must come over for dinner sometime and I'll show my pictures. So, have you been into Ganges?"

"Oh, yes."

"What do you think of it?"

"The village is looking better—with all the new shops. We won't have to go to Victoria anymore to get supplies."

"Yah, yah, that's right, but the parking is horrible. And did you see all the B.T.s?"

"What do you mean, B.T.s?" I asked.

"BLOODY TOURISTS!"

At the end of the summer, a couple of weeks before our return to California, Carrie Louise called on the phone. She sounded worried.

"I know yo'all are leavin' soon. I sure hate to see you go."

"Aren't you sweet, Carrie," I replied.

"Before you go, I think you better find someone else to look over your place, even though you're not rentin' it anymore. It's been hard for Cyril to do much for you the last few years. He isn't as strong as he used to be...and I can't trust him...I never know what he's goin' to do next."

"I know you've been concerned about him."

"I have a hunch he might have had a little stroke or somethin'. Anyway, don't tell him I've called you. Just go ahead and find someone else, then break the news to him. I think it's for the best."

I hung up the phone and told Maurie the news. "Question is—who should we get?" I asked.

"You know the marina just down the harbour from us?"

"Yes," I answered. "The Royal Vancouver Yacht Club bought it a couple of years ago."

"Yeah, it's a satellite marina for the use of Royal Van members." Maurie said. "Anyway, remember that fellow we met—Jim Ballantyne?"

"Yes. Isn't he the manager of the outstation?"

"Maybe he could help us. I think his house is on the hill just above us."

"He'd certainly be close by to watch over things," I replied. "Why don't you give him a call?"

So it was that Jim Ballantyne entered our lives, knocking one day on our kitchen door.

"I understand you want me to help with your house while you're away," he said. Jim was tall in stature, big and broad. His curly black hair dusted with gray; his dark eyes accentuated with heavy black brows; his jaw jutting with firmness.

"Yes, come in, come in, Jim" Maurie answered. "Glad to see you. How about a drink and we'll talk about it. What would you like?"

"Scotch would be fine—single malt if you've got it."

"No single malt, but I have Scotch," Maurie answered.

"Then pour it neat."

We settled down in our living room with the gray dusk hovering outside the cathedral windows. "Where do you hail from, Jim?" I asked.

"From Bradford, Ontario," Jim paused, "I was born at an early age." His dark eyes danced with devilment, watching my reaction.

This man has a sense of humour.

"Then my family moved to Scotland in '38 when I was nine years old, just before the war. We were caught there during the war and didn't return to Canada until '47."

"I understand you're a retired R.C.M.P.," Maurie said, handing a drink to Jim, then pouring one for himself.

"Indeed I am. Twenty-five years of service. In Saskatoon, the Northwest Territories, Ottawa, Edmonton, Alberta and Brandon, near Winnipeg. I retired out of the Burnaby Detachment."

"How on earth did you get to Salt Spring?" I asked.

"After I retired, I interviewed with the yacht club in Vancouver to be the manager for their Long Harbour outstation. They hired me. So, in 1980, Sandi, that's my wife, and I came over to the island. We bought the house just above you—it was unfinished on the inside, so I set to finishing it."

"I've never known a R.C.M.P. before," I said. "I'm curious. Did you really ride horses?"

"No, but I groomed them for review. And when the mares were in heat, it was bloody awful to keep the stallions in line. Which reminds me. What is the only animal that has an ass in the middle of its back?"

Maurie shot a funny look at me, "I don't know."

Here comes another joke.

"A horse for the Royal Canadian Mounted Police." Jim gave a high-pitched giggle.

This guy is a character. "So you didn't ride horses, but did you run any dog sleds?" I asked.

"Yes, along the Mackenzie River. My circuit included Great Slave Lake where I had to deal with the Indian tribes like the Slaveys, the Nahannis, the Rabbitskins. Oh, and the Chipweyans and Dogribs. The Indians weren't hospitable a-tall. In the summer I had to check on their activities from a river scow or canoe. See the colour on the back of my neck?" Jim gave a broad grin. "It's red!"

Maurie smiled to himself. "That wasn't much Scotch, Jim. How about another dash?"

"That would be nice," Jim replied.

I had become intrigued with Jim's stories. "Did anything dangerous happen to you?"

"One time I hit overflow ice."

"What's that?"

"It's water that freezes between two layers of ice— the surface looks solid, but it's easy to fall through. I was running my sled with the dogs across the river, traveling near a place called Two Mountains, when the ice caved in."

"What did you do?"

"First thing was to get the hell out of the water and get to shore. I stripped off my clothes and was bald naked in water 30 degrees below zero. Clothes freeze quickly in that temperature. They get heavy and you can drown in a matter of minutes. Fortunately the sled didn't sink. I pulled myself out of the water, dried quickly, and put on an extra pair of clothes—I always carried extra clothing on my sled. That was the closest call I ever had."

The sky darkened with a hint of Vancouver lights looming up behind Maracaibo. Jim's tales and jokes seemed endless. "Do you know what the dyslexic agnostic said?" Jim asked.

Maurie and I shook our heads and we both said, "No, what?"

"Is there really a DOG?" Out of Jim's wide mouth came a big giggle.

Maurie and I laughed, totally entertained.

"Where did you meet your wife?" I asked.

"Sandi? In the Northwest Territories—when I was stationed at Fort Reliance and she was close-by, about 300 miles."

"300 miles is close-by?"

Jim's eyes twinkled. "Sure, there's wide open spaces up there. She was a nurse in Yellowknife and that's where I met and married her. You'll have to meet her sometime. During the day she's in our house to cook meals while I work at the Royal Van. Then, at night, we both live at the outstation."

By now, the Scotch was running in the men's veins, allowing strangers to become friends. "I'll be happy to help you folks with the house," Jim said. "Just tell me what you want me to do."

"Good," Maurie replied, "I think we need another drink while we talk things over. And next time you stop in, I'll have some single malt for you."

18

THERE'S NO SUCH WORD AS FAIL

Jim Ballantyne tossed a black garbage bag full of dead wasps into the back of his pick-up truck—it was a fitting shroud for the pests. He braved our storage room to eliminate a nasty wasp nest growing larger by the day on the storage wall. With speed and insecticide spray, Jim attacked the crawling mass, then quickly covered the asphyxiated wasps with the garbage bag before they knew what hit them. With the black bag dispatched in the truck bed, he hesitated as he opened the truck door. There was a smirk on his face. He was about to say something. "Your house is a second home all right." Then came his big smile. "Everything is second-hand and falling apart."

Maurie half-laughed. "You're right, Jim, we've owned the place sixteen years and we've done very little to it. When we first bought the house, we couldn't afford to do much...that's why we rented it. Then, we put it up for sale and didn't touch it for several years."

"It's time to fix 'er up," the ex-sergeant commanded. "Rain leaked through the knothole in your bathroom and I plugged that up. Rain trails down the overhang near the kitchen door. You really need a new roof."

Jim had conscientiously watched over our house for a year and he soon learned of it deficiencies. "Come here, Maurie, I want you to look at the deck." The two men walked toward the house.

My mind, drifting, settled on an image of Jim in his R.C.M.P. dress uniform—a dashing figure, like the picture of the R.C.M.P. on a calendar that he had given to us. His red serge tunic—the colour evolving from the red coats of Britain—was trimmed with navy blue epaulets on each shoulder. His thick neck rose from a high collar trimmed with navy blue and festooned with R.C.M.P. insignias. A Sam Browne belt, holding a holster and a yellow lanyard connected to his gun, was tightly cinched at the waist. A leather strap crossed diagonally from his belt across his broad chest. The navy blue riding breeches, with a gold stripe along the length of his legs, fit without a wrinkle. Leather boots and gloves, tan Stetson hat, pointed at the crown, made it an impressive uniform, full of authority.

It was great fun knowing a real R.C.M.P. Jim was proud of his twenty-five year career. "Maintain the Right" was the R.C.M.P. motto printed boldly on the calendar and he lived by that.

An islander once said to me, "Ah, an R.C.M.P. is just a cop with a fancy uniform." He failed to realize that the uniform was so Canadian, symbolic of the country, unique in all its trappings.

Jim's loud voice from the deck abruptly brought me back to the present.

"Parts of your red pine deck are sagging with dry rot. It's getting dangerous, Maurie. They should be replaced."

Maurie looked at the boards and sighed. "Yes, I know. I guess it's time to do something." There was hesitation in his voice. I knew he was considering the costs involved. There was a long silence as Maurie took off his glasses and rubbed his eyes.

"Are you people aware that there's going to be a new government tax?" Jim asked.

Maurie put his glasses back on with a surprised look. "We're already paying a 7% tax on everything."

"Yeah, that's the P.S.T.—the Provincial Sales Tax, " Jim said, "but Ottawa doesn't give a fiddler's fart about the provincial tax. The government wants more money for its bloody programs ."

"What will the new tax be?" Maurie asked.

"Get ready for an additional 7% starting sometime next year."

"Whoa," Maurie said.

"Yep, it's going to be called the G.S.T."

"What does G.S.T. stand for?" I asked.

"General Services Tax." Jim laughed and looked at Maurie. "Even lawyers will have to add the G.S.T. to their bills."

"So, that will add up to 14% tax altogether." Maurie looked at me. "Geez, maybe we ought to start seriously thinking about doing the repairs before the new tax."

"While we're at it, we should paint the house," I said. "Look, the eaves are peeling and the green colour has faded."

"Why not, now's the time to do it," Jim said as he turned and headed back toward his truck.

Maurie called out to him, "I've got some single malt in the cupboard, Jim. Why don't you stay awhile and tell us your latest jokes?"

Jim climbed inside the truck and stuck his head out the window. "Not now, I still have chores to do for the yacht club." He paused, "Did you hear about the fella who thought 'harass' was two words?" He shot his broad smile at us and waved as he pulled out of our driveway.

In 1989 our financial circumstances were better. Maurie's legal practice had prospered; there was no need for me to teach, so I had resigned. That summer we seriously considered doing the improvements and received several bids. Fortunately, more workers were available on the island in the late 1980's.

Toward the end of the summer, Maurie said, "I've been thinking, Jacque, why don't we get that carpenter from New Zealand, who had the lowest bid, to replace only the upper deck, since we don't use the lower deck much."

"Great," I answered. "And he should rebuild the outside stairs too. That hippy-looking roofer comes highly recommended. Should we ask him to do the roof?."

"Yeah, let's make arrangements before we leave," Maurie said.

Hallelujah! I thought and got on the phone right away to call the workmen. Then I telephoned Jim.

Jim sounded happy at the news. "That roofer's a good one. Our neighbour, Phil Hume, made a suggestion."

"Oh, yeah?" I said. "He's a contractor. What did he suggest?"

"Phil thinks two skylights—one over your kitchen and one over your living room, near the fireplace—would bring in more light. Those cedar walls make the rooms pretty dark. He'd be happy to work with the roofer."

"That's a good idea. Let me run the thought past Maurie. Maybe Phil can come over and give us an estimate."

"By the way," Jim said, "Sandi and I want you and Maurie to come to supper before you leave for the summer. How about tomorrow night?"

"Great. I'd appreciate that. We have so many things to do before we head for San Diego." I hung up, remembering the wonderful dinners at the Cunninghams. They were getting older and it was difficult for them to do much. *But, in their place there's Thea Van Meel, the Blacks and now Jim and Sandi Ballantyne...how fortunate we are to have them all.*

The view from the Ballantyne's home, perched on the hill overlooking our maple trees and our roof-top, gave a broad vista of Scott Point. Their small, two-story house that Jim had finished on the inside was homey and comfortable. Sandi Ballantyne met us at the front door with a cheery smile and led us by the kitchen full of tasty aromas... and past her apple pies.

"Sandi" was an appropriate name for Jim's wife for her reddish-blonde hair accentuated her fair English complexion. She was a tall woman with an erect posture. I realized as we talked that Sandi, having a nursing background, was quite knowledgeable about medical procedures as well as home remedies. She seemed a competent person.

"Let's pour a drink," Jim said, "then I'll take you folks out to my special cabin next to the house."

Sandi laughed. "He likes to show off all his stuff from his R.C.M.P. days."

Jim's special cabin had a woodsy look, smelling of pine and leather upon entering. It was a mini-R.C.M.P. museum with walls displaying pictures, pistols, leather holsters, calendars and chevrons. A large photograph of mustachioed Jim in his dress uniform caught Maurie's attention.

"Hey, you were a handsome devil with that mustache," Maurie said teasingly.

"That's when I was younger, in the 1960s," Jim blushed. "But I want you to know that I won a competition with my design for that mace I'm holding. And I presented it to the Governor General at the Territorial Council meeting for the Yukon."

"Good for you," I said, " but what in the heck is a mace?"

Sandi answered my question. "It's an ornamental staff that represents the Queen at all official governmental functions. It must be present before the meeting can take place."

Jim showed off his bag pipes.

"I used to be a drummer in a pipe band when I was young," Jim explained. "Now I'm learning to play the bag pipe. Another fella and I go over to Duncan once a week to practice and perform."

"So this is where the pipe music comes from," I said. We often heard bag pipe music drift merrily over the trees and encircle our house, sometimes with a squeak or two.

"My dream is to form a pipe band on Salt Spring some day. In the meantime I have to practice." Jim laughed, "See the jowls I'm developing?" He puffed out his neck.

Maurie joked, "You look like a quivering bull frog, Jim." We all laughed.

"No more Scotch for you, Watson," Jim said. "Let's go have our supper."

Maurie downed the last bite of Sandi's delicious pie and announced, "Jim, we've got the New Zealander signed up to do a new deck for us."

"Is Phil going to help you with anything?" Jim asked.

"Yep. Phil will get together with the roofer and they'll start work on the roof and skylights as soon as we leave the island."

"You won't regret it, Maurie." Jim said. "They're both excellent."

"And, we're coming back in October to check on completion of the roof and to see the progress on the deck," Maurie added. "The carpenter wants to finish the job by November, so he can go back home to New Zealand."

"Well, Sandi, I think we should toast the Watsons for making their house a beautiful spot to gaze upon."

Our glasses clinked in celebration. It was a happy moment...which inspired Jim to regale us with his poetry :

> "There was a maid
> Down in the glade
> In times quite medieval.
> A traveler aspied her
> And plied her with cider
> And now she's
> The forest's prime evil."

We flew to the island in October for a few days of inspection. The new composition shingles, covering the damage from Haddon's lounge chairs, neatly framed the skylights. Inside the house, the skylights were picture windows to the sky. Rays of warm sunshine filtered through them during the daytime. When I looked to the world above, I saw tree tops swaying in the breeze. We didn't turn on a light until the dusk faded. At night the moon and stars sparkled behind ghostly clouds.

The rotten decks were torn down and the lumber stacked in the driveway. The New Zealander bent over his buzz saw, steadily cutting cedar planks, then hammering them into place over the posts and beams. He set panels of glass horizontally along the edge of the deck which were framed with cedar 2 by 4's; the glass panels replaced the old style pickets. Finally he nailed a railing of 2 by 6's five inches above the panels. The harbour looked magnified through the stylish glass screens.

The carpenter worked in the rain, trying to meet his deadline before his departure from the island. The deck was not quite finished when we left, but he assured us, "Listen, luvs, your deck will be finished in good time. Now go on home and don't be bothered."

I returned to the island again in the spring and found our freshly built deck to be a natural appendage to our house. My mission on this short trip was to hire a painter. After several estimates and recommendations, I made my choice. I didn't hire the usual male painter in white coveralls, but a young single mother in Levis who asked to bring her child to play while she worked. Earning a living as a single parent and supporting a child is not an easy task. I admired her doing a man's job so I hired her. I watched her work for a few days. She delicately applied the fresh coat of forest green paint with precision. There was hardly a drip. And her child played contentedly by himself.

I had grown weary of packing up our dirty duds, driving into the village and waiting to use the coin operated washing machines. Innumerable hours and coins were spent on this inconvenient chore. Even in the new laundry, odors of sweat and grim were still present. Fear of having our clothes stolen made me sit nervously with a watchful eye on the machines.

Enough of this laundry drudgery, I came to the conclusion. *If we're spending money on improving the house, a new washer and dryer would be a great improvement too.*   So, I called Sears in Victoria and ordered a washer and dryer. Two white, magnificent machines were delivered bearing English and French instructions. What a delight to have the sweet smells of detergent and bleach when doing the laundry at home. How relaxing to sort the clothes in piles spread out on the floor where nobody would snitch them.

Our timing was perfect for all improvements were completed before the new tax went into effect. One morning I perched on a rock near the edge of the harbour and gazed up at our house on the bank above.

I feel so proud of the way the house looks now. It's better than ever. I remember how appealing it was when we first bought it. I called it our "dream house" and what a nightmare it became with the fire. Mom and Dad saved it for us. And so did the Cunninghams. So many tenants have lived in it—if only the walls could talk. What fun we've had with our houseguests and our Mexican parties. And we kicked Haddon out. Not without sacrifice. Thank God the house didn't sell. Jim has been a godsend. He's as dogged as "Clancy of the Mounted Police," from Robert Service's poem. How does that line go? "...there's no such word as 'fail.'"

19

ISLAND RELIC

Island Car was still a disgrace. Our buggy became more dilapidated as the years rolled by. Rust continued to advance over its fenders and doors like an incurable disease. Every time we parked the car in the village, hippies looked at it with envy, coveting it. Each summer Jim struggled with charging the battery to get the car started before our arrival. "What a bloody heap," he would say, kicking the tired tires.

But the corroded little motor kept running. Maurie made sure of that. Whenever a mechanical problem arose, he took Island Car to be doctored by Richard Murakami, an island mechanic.

Murakami, as he was called by islanders, hailed from a Japanese family that settled on the island years ago. The family labored diligently to develop their vegetable farm and chicken pens. Unfortunately, in the spring of 1942, after the Japanese attacked Pearl Harbour, the Murakamis and other Japanese throughout the west and northwest, were ordered by the federal governments of United States and Canada to move into "relocation centers." The family endured the ordeal of internment. When they came back to Salt Spring after the war, they discovered all their property and belongings were gone. Like many Japanese, the Murikamis started building their farm and their lives over again.

The Murakami home was located on Rainbow Road, outside of Ganges Village. The driveway looked like the aftermath of a demolition derby with a line of injured cars awaiting repair. Two cavernous garages at the end of the driveway housed cars delicately balanced on hoists, cars half sprayed with paint, cars mangled and twisted. Automobiles surrounded the house, parked in the weeds looking like old relics. In the nearby yard, Richard's widowed mother, Mrs. Murakami, sat on a motorized wheelchair surveying the mechanics as they scurried from car to car.

Murakami always greeted us with an impish grin; I think it amused him to work on our old car. He said to Maurie, "Here comes the millionaire from California who drives an old car."

If we were millionaires, Island Car would have disappeared long ago, I said to myself.

"What's the problem this time?" asked Murakami, his wise eyes peering from behind his glasses.

"We were driving in Victoria yesterday and this strange screeching noise started beneath the hood," Maurie answered.

Murakami unlatched the hood and peered inside. When he bent over, his rainbow coloured suspenders stretched tightly from his low slung work pants. A portable phone poked out of his back pocket. He was a short man, round and soft like a marshmallow, with shortly cropped black hair.

"It's a wonder you made it back to the island, Mr. Watson," Murakami said, "your water pump is about to blow." He raised his head from beneath the hood. "Want me to call Victoria and order a new one?"

"By all means," Maurie answered.

Murakami pulled out his portable phone and chattered to some auto parts dealer, then hung up. "You can't drive it another inch...you'll have to leave it here."

"But my wife and I were going shopping in the village," Maurie said. "We have no car."

"Take mine. Keep it 'til late tomorrow when your Chevy will be ready. Here are the keys."

Maurie looked at the keys in his hand, then smiled at Murakami, "That's very kind of you. We wouldn't be treated like this in the states."

"You're welcome, Mr. Watson. Now, I gotta go." Murakami dashed off to help a mechanic at the end of the driveway with another problem.

One spring, my San Diego friend Marijeanne Crabtree and I flew to Canada while Maurie was on a fishing trip in the United States. We enjoyed relaxing on the island. Later in the week, I wanted to show her Butchart Gardens and Victoria. So we climbed in Island Car and boarded the ferry at Fulford Harbour bound for Swartz Bay. A constable waved our car over as we debarked the ferry.

"What does that R.C.M.P. want?" I asked Marijeanne.

"I don't know, but you better drive carefully between those red cones he's pointing to."

"This is a road check, Madam. The officious constable said. "May I see your registration, driver's license and insurance papers?"

I handed over the papers indignantly, claiming the car was imported and everything was in order. Inwardly, I became nervous over what he might find.

"Turn on your lights, please. Left signal, please. Right signal. Brake lights. Turn your steering wheel, please. Try your windshield wipers. Let's look under the hood," came the list of commands.

Then the constable issued his ultimatum. "Madam, I'm writing you a notice to register your car in British Columbia with Canadian insurance within seven working days."

"But that's impossible. I'm here for three more days and tomorrow is the only working day left."

"Sorry, Madam. I'm also writing you up for a deficient right headlight and a cracked windshield, both of which must be repaired. If you don't take care of these matters, a sizeable fine will follow. Go to the nearest R.C.M.P. Detachment."

"Where is it?"

"Sidney. You're excused, Madam."

I was seething. "What an arrogant cuss," I said to
Marijeanne. "All the years with California plates
seemed acceptable. Now our plans for a leisurely day
seeing the gardens and Victoria will turn into a day
battling Canadian bureaucracy."

I found the R.C.M.P. Detachment in Sidney and
went straight into the office. The office was decorated
in bureaucratic drabness, smelling of stale papers. I
explained my plight to the officer in charge. He agreed
to delay the issue of plates until the following summer
since the car was registered in Maurie's name and he
was not in Canada. However, the constable insisted that
I fix the headlight and windshield and gave me directions to the nearest garage.

The front headlight was easily replaced. The garage
couldn't help me with the windshield. I called
Murakami on the island, told him about my predicament
and asked, "How much will it cost to replace the
cracked windshield...and how long will it take?"

I heard Murakami walking with his portable phone.
"Mrs. Watson, I know it will take at least three days to
find a windshield. Now, let me see what my parts book
says about windshields." There was a rifling of pages.
"It will cost...let me see... $585 Canadian."

"There's NO WAY I'm going to pay $585 for a
windshield. We only paid $50 for the clunker," I told
him and hung up.

"Marijeanne, I'm going right back to that R.C.M.P.
Detachment in Sidney and plead my case," I said in total
exasperation.

The officer was out of the office, but luckily his secretary listened to my story and she seemed sympathetic.

"Let me see this car," she said as she walked out the office door to the parking lot.

She chuckled to herself when she looked at it. "My, my." She shook her head. "Whoever wrote you up was a real chicken shit," she said. "Your car is operable within standards. You've repaired the headlight. The windshield crack is negligible and on the passenger side. I'll waive the notice for windshield repair on the computer. However, you must get B.C. plates and B.C. insurance this coming summer. And NEVER, NEVER take this car off Salt Spring Island again."

One evening, while driving home after dinner at Migs and Wes', an R.C.M.P. police car shone its spotlight on Island Car and made us pull over. I was in the driver's seat and shuddered to myself, *Oh, no. I hope we're not in trouble again.*

The officer pointed his flashlight into my face, then into Maurie's. "Do you know you were weaving on Long Harbour Road?"

"Officer, don't worry. There's a lot of play in this old steering wheel," I smiled, hoping his light wouldn't catch the cracked windshield.

"All right, Miss, but stay on your side of the road," he admonished me. And he let us go.

I felt SO relieved. "Maybe he thought he was apprehending a drunk driver," I giggled to Maurie.

The blue tank still trundles along the forest roads. How many miles have we put on it over the years? Who knows...the odometer is broken!

20

GOLF IS A FOUR LETTER WORD

It was a decision made too late in life—to play golf, that is. Since Maurie was nearing retirement age and we had more free time, our thought was to try a new sport. Not knowing what headaches and backaches lay ahead, Maurie and I innocently bought new clubs and took golf lessons. Flailing with frustration, we started on the long path of trying to hit the little white ball. We mustered the pluck to join the Salt Spring Golf and Country Club, a regulation, nine-hole course, which could be played twice as eighteen holes.

It was a challenging course, located near Portlock Park. Broad, green fairways over undulating hills were carved out of the forest. The property was originally owned by a black settler from California, a Mr. Armstead Buckner. Through an agent in Victoria, The Reverend Edward Wilson, an Anglican minister on the island from 1894-1909, purchased 40 hectares (one hectare equals approximately 2 1/4 acres) with bush and swamp and a rickety old log house with a mud chimney. He transplanted his two-room house from Victoria, set it on the property and enlarged the home, calling it Barnsbury. With time, the rector developed orchards, meadows of cattle and fields for crops. In 1928, a golf club was formed by fourty-four people wanting to play on the Barnsbury Estate, then owned by Wilson's son, Norman. Legend has it that the first greens were made of sand and that the first golf was played among sheep who mowed the grass. Norman Wilson turned from farming the property to managing the golf course. The family home became the clubhouse; unfortunately it was demolished by fire in 1959. Islanders formed a holding company in 1961 to finance the purchase of the property for a golf club. A new clubhouse was built in 1963. Gordon Fergusson was the first golf pro, hired in 1987.

Our logic for joining the club, which in 1989 required a modest initiation fee and yearly non-resident dues, was that it was inexpensive compared to private clubs in California. There were no tee times—unheard of in San Diego. Members could play nine or eighteen holes—even take a lunch break after the first nine. This was our kind of golf club, we thought.

Archie and Kas Black were brave enough to take us for our first nine holes of golf at our new club. It must have been a trying experience for them to play with two bumblers. They were old-time members of the club who served on a committee that developed a watering system to green the fairways.

Maurie stepped up to the first tee and took a practice swing. I held my breath. To my relief he hit a nice shot with great distance. At the height of the drive, however, the ball seemed mysteriously pulled to the right, like by a magnet, and it disappeared into the trees.

"You hit your ball in 'Tiger Country,'" Archie said. "Those are terrible conditions over there."

Maurie scrambled down the fairway and into the trees. He raked the leaves with his club, looking for his ball. Kind Archie joined in the search, but no luck. Maurie shrugged his shoulders and tossed another ball out onto the fairway. Poor guy. He lost a total of thirteen balls that day while playing nine holes.

"Take a mulligan." Archie suggested after I blooped the ball a few yards off the second tee.

"What's that?" I asked, feeling ignorant.

"It means you can hit a second ball."

Arch and Kas consistently hit the ball straight down the fairway, much to my envy. They pitched onto the green with accuracy and putted into the hole with ease. Archie smiled after the first hole. "Drive for show, putt for dough."

"Don't roll your pull cart on the apron of the green," Kas cautioned me on the third hole, "you folks have to learn golf etiquette." I felt uneasy not knowing the do's and don'ts of the game. The Blacks invited us to play several times, while drumming the rules into our heads.

Then there were the resident Canadian geese feeding on the fairways. These critters never flew south because the picking was too good on the course. Hitting a ball and avoiding the small flock was almost impossible. Finally, large plastic eagles, standing three feet high, were placed strategically around the course and rid golfers of the pests.

If anything can make you feel stupid it's golf, particularly when you start mingling with golfers who know what they're doing. I joined the ladies nine-hole golf group at the club thinking it would be a good experience to play once a week with other people and it would improve my game. To my surprise, I received a trophy after my first nine-hole round—for hitting the ball into the most bunkers (sandtraps). The captain handed me a porcelain figurine of a golfer with his bottom in the air and his nose in the bunker, eyeballing the golf ball.

"You can keep this prize for a week," the captain said with smile, "put it on your mantle, but be sure to bring it back." I heard snickers in the clubhouse when she handed it to me. Fortunately there was no mantle in our island house.

Every Wednesday morning I joined the nine-holers to hack, hook, bash and slice that elusive ball. During one round, I played with an attractive woman named Ann McLeod who seemed quite intent on her game. Ann was my age, a pretty woman with a pleasant smile. We introduced ourselves on the first tee. I liked her immediately.

"Where do you live on the island?" I asked her after we teed off. That was one of my standard questions when playing with a stranger.

"We have a house on Maracaibo," Ann answered. "We bought the lot several years ago, then built after Gundy retired." She walked over to her second shot and hit. "Gundy's my husband. Where do you live?"

"On Scott Point, overlooking Long Harbour," I answered and took my second shot. We walked over a rise, then proceeded down a long stretch that eventually led to a 5-par hole at the bottom of the first fairway. Because golfers couldn't see over the rise for their second shots, a bell post stood to the right of the fairway, three-quarters of the way down; golfers, after their third shots or whatever, were to ring the bell signaling golfers behind it was safe to take their shots.

"What kind of work did your husband do?" My second standard question.

"He was a chartered accountant in Vancouver and Saskatoon. Now that we're settled on the island, he wants me to take up golf." Ann addressed her third shot and hit. "He's really a good golfer."

It was my turn to hit. "What's his handicap?" I asked, starting my backswing.

"Six."

My arms froze in mid-air. *Six! What a LOW handicap.* The shock jolted through my body, causing me to slice the ball off to the right and it rolled behind the bell post. To cover up my embarrassment, I clowned around struggling to remove the bell post, knowing full well I couldn't. It brought a laugh. Then I ungraciously straddled the bell post and tapped my ball, only to see it dribble a few feet down the fairway. In a sulk I rang the bell.

"Oh, the joys of golf," I said sarcastically, grinding my teeth. My score on the first hole was a disaster.

We walked along, becoming better acquainted, pulling our golf carts in the bright sunshine, traipsing up and down the emerald green fairways edged by the forest. I admired the colourful golfing outfits worn by the Canadian ladies, such as the "plus fours" which were knickers with long socks. I watched them inch along the fairways in the distance, their clubs glinting in the sunlight as they swung at the ball. Occasionally a lady would wave and call a greeting to Ann. I was envious that she knew so many people.

"Why don't we get our husbands together and play this week?" Ann suggested at the end of our round. I swallowed hard and accepted her offer, more out of appreciating her friendliness than wanting to play golf.

Our day to play with the McLeods arrived. Gundy McLeod stood as tall as Maurie. He was a trim, sixty-year-old fellow with a ruddy complexion and reddish hair. Gundy extended his big hand to Maurie. "Hi, I'm Gundy McLeod."

"Hello," Maurie said, shaking his hand. "I'm Maurie Watson and this is my wife, Jackie."

"You certainly have an unusual name," I said.

"It's a nickname for Gordon. Maurie, shall we tee off?"

Gundy played masterfully. Ann concentrated with full attention on improving her game. We, as usual, floundered around. However, it was the beginning of a new friendship.

Many couples on the island, such as the McLeods, had previously known each other while growing up in Vancouver or attending the University of British Columbia. Now, retired and transplanted, they renewed their old friendships. Joining the Salt Spring Golf and

Country Club was one way to become acquainted on the island. We were newcomers to the golfing scene and felt slightly awkward not knowing many people...and certainly not knowing golf. But we climbed into our golfing clothes, threw our golf bags over our shoulders and put on a happy smile.

Maintaining a handicap took effort. Every time we played golf, we saw Gundy either practicing or playing. Later we learned he had been playing since he was eleven years old. We also discovered he was the president of the 400-member club. Needless to say, he was a bit ahead of us.

There were competitions and cups for both men and women. Each year we noticed improvements to the club: bright flowers planted near the tees, a new cart shed, berms separating the fairways, elevated tees and greens.

Ann switched to the ladies eighteen hole group and I screwed up my courage a few years later to do the same. I knew I would be with the big girls and I quaked in my cleats at the thought of it. Every Tuesday morning, I nervously joined the intense ladies as they prepared their carts and scorecards. I marched out on the fairway with them, feeling like I was about to do battle—only with a little white ball. *What am I doing here?* I asked myself. My angst traveled down my arms into my club and out my swing. My ball seemed to land under trees, on ground under repair, in the pond and in the rough.

To be in the company of some excellent golfers was a learning experience; their long drives, skilled pitches and cautious putting taught me how the game should be played. I overheard them talking to each other without the slightest idea of what they meant: "That was a good bogie." "She whiffed the ball." "That was a good up and a good down." "It's within the leather."

They tolerated me, wondering who the interloper was. They called me Jean and Joyce, everything but my name. I smiled and tagged along, learned the etiquette, tried to fit in, never mentioned my high handicap. I practiced on the driving range, even played nine holes by myself many times in hopes of improving. But, in my heart, I knew I had a long way to go. It would take time and practice. I wasn't sure I'd live long enough to perfect my golfing skills.

Maurie and I became better acquainted with golfers each summer through "Twilight Mixers." At 4:30 P.M., three or four times each summer, nine holes of golf were played by mixed groups of husbands and wives. Drinks and dinner followed in the club house and prizes were awarded. We began to know some people on a first name basis. The most encouraging guy in the club was Gordie Fergusson, the golf pro. He was always happy to see us and made us feel comfortable.

I persevered with golf and something unexpected happened. Not lowering my handicap, but making new friends. Ladies said "hello" to me in the grocery store. Sometimes I was asked to play during the week. A small group of women invited me to have an informal lunch and play nine holes on Friday afternoons. All had different handicaps yet each had the same friendly ways. My uneasiness faded. Some good shots came. I even won a prize for low net. But the best part came when they called me by my name.

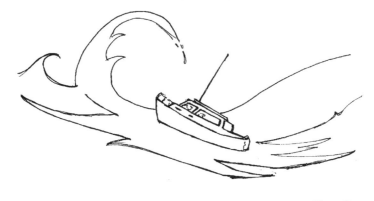

21

BOAT FEVER

The passing parade of sloops and ketches, motor yachts and sport fishing boats floating up and down Long Harbour made us drool. Maurie looked wistfully at the yachts through his binoculars. Some boats were searching for a quiet cove to drop anchor, some headed for the Royal Van outstation, others beelined it to the Maracaibo docks. Yachts, festooned with Canadian and American flags and small bright burgees, looked dressed up for a holiday. And it was a holiday—all summer long. Once, a long sleek yacht carrying a couple of speed boats and a helicopter motored by; we stood in awe of the floating wealth.

We wanted to be on the water again too. Our old motorboat had quickly sold in 1982 when we listed our house. How we envied Migs and Wes with their Double Eagle boat—a Canadian inboard runabout. They always gave us a beep with their boat horn when on their way for a picnic lunch near one of the islands. We watched the Beckmanns zip by in their boat usually overflowing with kids, sometimes pulling a water-skier.

Maurie got the boat bug bad in 1989 and started poring over boating magazines. He searched and researched boats for a year. He dragged me to boat shows where we crawled every which-way to inspect the merits of each craft.

"What do you think of this one?" he asked. "I want a fishing boat I can trailer behind our Jeep—one that doesn't cost an arm and leg." (In 1988 we bought a new Jeep Cherokee.) I was more interested in comfortable sleeping quarters and a galley.

Finally, after much looking, we decided on a 22 foot C-Dory Cruiser. "The 22' planes clean at 10 knots!" the brochure claimed.

Maurie and Jim Reynolds, our yachtsman friend, drove from San Diego in the summer of 1990, picked up our C-Dory in Kent, Washington where she was built and trailered her to the island. Joan Reynolds and I flew to Canada ahead of time to meet the fellows upon their arrival.

It was exciting to hear our Jeep pull in the driveway late one night. We ran outside the house to see the arrival of our new boat.

Maurie jumped out the car, acting like a kid with a new toy. "Isn't she beautiful?" He proudly ran his hands along her lightweight molded hull of fiberglass, hand laid over a balsa core. He pointed to the broad navy blue band that ran smartly along each side of her hull; her cabin was trimmed in blue as well.

"Climb aboard and let's celebrate the arrival of our new C-Dory," Maurie called out. He helped us step onto the trailer fender and over the starboard gunnel down into her cockpit. A 70-horse power Johnson motor, an 8-horse Johnson auxiliary motor and a swim step were mounted on the transom. He pointed to the automatic water pump near the cabin door. "It's self-bailing. Come, see the cabin."

Maurie and Jim ducked their big frames under the cabin entry and we followed them. Inside there were two V berths in the bow with a privacy curtain and a porta-potty. A dinette, which could convert into a berth, was on the port side. On the starboard were the pilot's seat and the galley which included a sink with a 16 gallon fresh-water supply, storage cabinets and a teak counter top. Aluminum-framed windows ringed the cabin.

"This boat looks super, Maurie." I said. "It'll be perfect for fishing." Jim Reynolds nodded his head in agreement.

"That's right, now follow me outside on the walk-around deck," Maurie said. "I've got a flashlight, but watch your step. This non-skid section alongside the cabin is narrow and has cleats."

We carefully walked forward on the port side holding onto teak handrails atop the cabin. Once on the bow, we stepped around a hatch and held on to a stainless steel handrail; an anchor was mounted on the bow with its chain disappearing into a storage locker below.

"Aren't we going to have fun?" I asked. "Now we can see all the Gulf Islands and the San Juans too."

"Absolutely, and Desolation Sound." Maurie slipped his arm around my waist and gently kissed me. "Now let's go back to the cabin and have a drink with the Jim and Joan."

Jim and Joan Reynolds stayed 10 days. Jim helped Maurie install a marine radio, aerial and depth sounder. They took us to task, grilling us on how to handle our new boat. Round and round we went, practicing, practicing, practicing. It seemed we docked a hundred times. Maurie learned the touch of the controls and I learned to throw the fenders over the sides and tie the lines. Their training paid off, for we felt comfortable with the boat upon their departure.

Her 22-foot length and 8-foot beam made her cozy, close and *somewhat* comfortable. Being two big people, we stepped on each other's feet, bumped into one another and knocked our heads on the low doorway. We toodled around the island, breaking in our sea legs and our boatsmanship.

Our first long trip was south to the San Juan Islands located across the Canadian-American border. All went smoothly until our return. We were coming from Orcas Island, crossing President's Channel and trying to get to South Pender Island. Our heading was north to north-westerly, close to the southeasterly side of Stuart Island. Suddenly, the boat came upon swirling tidal rips which are caused when two fast-moving currents collide during a tidal change. Wind and whitecaps buffeted us about. Maurie held onto the wheel as the boat thrashed around in the turbulent water. Pots and pans banged in the cabinets; bottles and jars rolled on shelves. The thudding and jarring didn't let up. It was frightening. My head began to throb. Maurie slowed the motor.

"Oops, watch out, here come some big waves," Maurie warned. A strong wind blew directly against the boat, whitecaps washed over the bow, spraying salt water across the cabin windows. The bow slapped down into a deep trough with a jarring thud.

"This is God-awful rough. I'm glad there's a water pump in the cockpit. The banging makes my head ache." Maurie braced his foot against the cabin floor just to stay in the pilot's seat.

In the distance we saw a speck of a boat disappearing behind a point of land.

"I wonder if there's a sheltered cove where that boat went," Maurie said. "I think we can make it over there." He headed the boat in the same direction, fighting the wind and tidal rips all the way. We continued to be bashed about. I held onto the kitchen table for dear life, praying we would make it. I tried to get our life vests out from beneath the seats, but I was knocked to the floor. The endless pounding continued. The point of land loomed closer. When we finally rounded the point, there lay a small, peaceful cove. What happy relief!

After dropping the anchor, we took two aspirin tablets and slept off our exhaustion for a couple of hours. Later, when the wind died, we slowly headed toward Long Harbour on rolling, glassy water. It was a long time before we entered President's Channel again and then it was with tide tables and proper charts.

There were other disasters, but all minor. One day I helplessly watched a bottle of red wine topple over from the counter and shatter on the floor, shooting glassy shards and red splotches every which-way in the cabin. "Oops!" I cried.

"You should NEVER put anything on the counter while we're under way," Maurie shouted angrily at me. "Look at this mess." He stopped the boat and stared at me in disgust. I sheepishly got out the bucket and sponge, knelt on my knees and carefully wiped up the splintered glass and wasted wine. It was a hard lesson learned.

Many times, Maurie's fanny bumped me as he leaned over to put something away. "Oops! 'Scuse me. Didn't mean to run into you."

I was suddenly inspired. "That's what we should name our boat."

"What do you mean?"

"*Oops*... it's a perfect name for our boat...we say it so much."

"That's a silly name...but it's kinda cute."

No other name seemed to fit. After owning her a year and more tiny disasters, we christened her *Oops*. Boaters smiled at our little *Oops* and waved to us from their big gorgeous yachts with names like *Urine the Money, Shirley's Temple, Queen of the C's,* and *Legal Ease.* "Why did you name 'er *Oops*?" they'd call out. Our standard answer: "We say *Oops* several times a a day for all the little accidents aboard."

At first, we trailered her between California and British Columbia so we could enjoy the boat in San Diego and on Salt Spring. However, bouncing along Interstate 5 for 1,400 miles trailing 3,400 pounds of boat soon became tedious. To avoid paying the high import tax on the boat in Canada if we kept it there, Maurie decided to store *Oops* in Anacortes, Washington during the year. It was a convenient place just below the Canadian border to pick up the boat as we drove north to catch a ferry to the island.

Later, in 1992, when we heard rumors about a moratorium on the building of docks on the island, we built a twenty-five foot dock in front of our house. We no longer had to walk over Thea Van Meel's property to get to our boat. Convenient steps were built down the bank to our dock. And the rock crab were abundant in the deep waters below.

After our encounter with President's Channel, we learned that *Oops'* bow couldn't take heavy chop so we waited for sunny days and smooth water to plane out of Long Harbour, speed by Prevost Island, pass through Navy Channel and head for Saturna Island where Maurie found a great fishing hole. I dare not divulge its location, but the setting was breath-taking.

The pale blue sky, painted with strokes of white clouds, contrasted with the deep, cobalt blue of the water. On the hazy skyline to the southeast, snow-capped Mount Baker dominated the setting. The sun sprinkled diamonds of light upon the water. Our boat quietly rocked, drifting slowly with the current; small waves slapped against its hull. *Oops* bobbed past rocks with clusters of seals sunning themselves; seagulls and cormorants dotted the islets; a bald eagle swooped by— its stunning white and black feathers created a sharp contrast against the pale sky. Echoes faintly crossed the water from the wash of waves against the shores of Saturna.

Maurie patiently jigged his rod up and down, up and down from the stern of the boat, hoping the flash of his Crocodile lure would attract a ling cod from deep below.

A uneventful half hour passed. I sat inside the cabin writing on my laptop computer.

"Quick, Jacque, get the net. I think I've got a big one," Maurie cried out.

I reached under the bow to get the net, ran out to the cockpit and stretched over the gunnel holding the net by its pole as he slowly reeled in. A speckled body gyrated close to the surface of the water, fighting Maurie's line all the way.

"He's big all right," Maurie said excitedly. "Now, when I bring him up to side of the boat, put the net under him."

This was not an easy task for the fish wriggled and splashed. He was so big, he didn't fit into the net.

"Forget the net. I'll just bring him into the stern on my line." The lure was hooked on the lip of the fish— he was struggling to dislodge it. Maurie flipped the fish into the boat. I jumped back in excitement and hit my head on the doorway. "Oops."

Maurie tried to remove the hook, but the fish slapped all over the cockpit. Finally, when the fish lay worn out, Maurie removed the hook by twisting it with his pliers. A huge, gaping mouth rimmed by scissor teeth looked up at him; its long speckled body seemed small in comparison to its cavernous mouth.

"It's a keeper. It measures just 70 centimeters. We'll have fish for dinner tonight." Maurie held up his catch by the gills and proudly smiled while I took his picture.

It became routine handling *Oops*—securing the lines, throwing out fenders and docking the boat. In order to go ashore, we purchased a red dinghy with oars; exploring and hiking on islands stretched our limbs and became the remedy for cabin fever. Like two dancers, we learned to shift and rotate around each other within the boat's tight surroundings. Being aboard *Oops* was like camping on the water—cooking with the portable butane stove, showering on the swim step with water warmed in the plastic sun shower, bedding down in sleeping bags for the night and, of course, spraying for mosquitoes To avoid clutter, everything had its place.

Our confidence grew each time we took *Oops* out on the water. Maurie operated the boat like an old salt. Scooting down to the San Juans in two hours and spending a few days exploring inlets and coves broadened our knowledge of the archipelago running between Canada and the United States.

The next year Maurie said, "I'm ready to put the boat and trailer on the ferry, go to Lund on the mainland, then launch the boat and cruise Desolation Sound for a week. What do you say?"

"You mean go 'gunkholing?'" I asked excitedly. "Gunkholing" was a term used by boaters for cruising among the islands, exploring bays and coves, then anchoring every night, sometimes in "gunk" or mud.

"Yeah. Let's watch the weather reports and when a stretch of good weather is predicted, let's be ready to go."

Desolation Sound was a boater's paradise with warm waterways, abundant wildlife, sheltered bays, numerous lakes and scenic waterfalls. Located about 90 miles north of Vancouver, its protected waters encompassed a conglomeration of different sized and shaped islands; some low-lying, others mountainous; some with good anchorages, others with rocky bottoms; some with deep inlets, others with sheer cliffs; some minuscule, others immense. From the Copeland Islands in the south to Stuart Island in the north from westerly Quadra Island to East Redonda Island, the exploring seemed endless.

Captain George Vancouver discovered the sound in the spring of 1792 during his exploration of British Columbia. In his journal, Vancouver wrote, "Our residence here was truly forlorn; an awful silence pervaded the gloomy forests." The islands and anchorages impressed him as being remote and silent; therefore, he named the area Desolation Sound.

What repelled Vancouver in 1792 attracts boaters from the Seattle and Vancouver areas today. Unfortunately, in their quest for beauty and tranquility, hundreds of boats invade Desolation Sound during the summertime. Boats overcrowd the more popular coves and the waters sometimes become polluted with sewage.

Avoiding the crowds became a challenge. We sought out lesser known coves like Galley Bay on Gifford Peninsula. Although it was a broad bay exposed from the north, the view of the majestic mountains on the mainland was spectacular, especially at sunset. The evening glow reflected on the snow-capped mountains anointing them in a rosy hue. Few boats dropped anchor there.

We didn't have sophisticated navigational equipment like Loran or GPS (Global Position System). All we had was a marine radio and a depth sounder. Reading the charts, sighting points of land and following the compass became crucial in knowing our position. Only a few times did we become confused in Desolation Sound.

Finding the opening to Von Donop Inlet on Cortez Island had us stumped. Coming along the western side of the island, we couldn't find the cleft that was supposed to be the entrance. Totally puzzled, we decided to catch up with a sizeable yacht cruising ahead and ask for directions.

The day was extremely hot, so the bare backs of two yachtsmen sitting on the flying bridge didn't seem unusual—their blonde hair was blowing in the breeze. *Oops* came up to the stern. Large gold letters announced the boat's name—*Ecstasy.* From the rear it looked to be a large and luxurious boat. Maurie approached the yacht on its port side, stuck his head out the cabin window and yelled up to the bridge, "Where's the entrance to Von Donop Inlet?"

The two yachtsmen turned toward him and asked, "What?"

Maurie removed his head from the window and gave me a strange look. "My God, one of 'em is a woman."

I peered out the window and there sat a bare, big-breasted woman, her sun-burned boobs pointed straight at Maurie.

"What did you say?" she yelled again. Her partner sported a blonde barrel chest.

Maurie paused, swallowed hard and sounded like he was strangled, "Where's Von Donop Inlet?"

They both stood up without a stitch on and pointed to the right. "It's just ahead," the bosomed lady shouted. Maurie became so distracted that he swerved off course and nearly rammed *Ecstasy* with our bow. This was our first exposure (no pun intended) to a certain liberated attitude that's common among boaters.

I was still laughing when he found the entrance. Slowing down, we cautiously cruised through the long, funnel-like opening. The end of the inlet was shaped like an arrowhead. We dropped anchor in the north hook where we would be sheltered from the winds.

Our custom was to explore in the dinghy after dinner, curiously rowing by beautiful yachts and ogling them. There floated *Ecstasy*, anchored in the south hook. All was battened down with nary a light. Maurie's quiet rowing gently rocked the yacht.

"Don't make waves," I whispered.

At the end of our Desolation Sound trip, we headed south toward Jarvis Inlet and Hotham Sound. Our destination—the Harmony Islands. What a beautiful setting—four small islands snuggled beneath waterfalls on the east side of the sound with delightful coves. Warm water, sometimes in the 70's, surrounded these islands—perfect for swimming. Oyster beds clung to the rocks, just for the picking.

Our first mistake was to arrive at the Harmonies late in the afternoon—after numerous boats had set anchor

and stern-tied for the night. Stern-tying means tying a
line from the stern of the boat to something stable on the
shore, like a tree or rock; this is done in addition to
dropping an anchor to prevent swinging of the boat.

For half an hour, Maurie struggled to secure the
anchor on the rocky bottom close to one of the islands.
I helped by backing *Oops* up and down between boats
anchored close by. Back and forth, back and forth we
went, not catching the bottom. I looked out the cabin
windows and realized we were the entertainment for the
cocktail hour. All eyes were upon us. Finally the
anchor caught and we had a good scope. Scope is the
amount of line and chain from the anchor to the boat.

Then came the stern-tying—which is an acquired
art. Maurie rowed ashore in the dinghy, carrying the
line with lots of slack. It's awkward to beach the
dinghy, step out of it, carry the line and keep your balance at the same time. He tried tying the line around
several trees before he found one that held the line
straight from the stern. His footing was shaky on the
slippery rocks. I prayed, *Dear God, I hope he doesn't
topple over getting into the dinghy with everyone watching.*

He made it safely back to the boat, but as he climbed
into the cockpit, the dinghy slipped away beneath his
feet. He grabbed the gunnel with both arms, his feet
dangling over the side in the water.

"Damn it, help me get in the boat," he shouted.
Maurie looked like a beached whale, half-way hanging
into the boat. I reached over the side and gave his
britches a big tug. He came sprawling into the boat,
head first.

How embarrassing.

Chagrined, Maurie was removing his wet boat shoes, mumbling swear words to himself, when a speedboat suddenly cruised alongside.

"We all watched you anchor your boat and it took you longer than it did us." There were two girls in the boat who appeared to be teenagers. The one driving the boat said, "My mother and father are sending you some wine and seafood linguini. They figure you need it about now, after all you went through." The other girl handed us two glasses of white wine, then plates of pasta.

"Thank you," I said. "Aren't you nice. Which is your boat?"

"It's over there," the driver pointed beyond our bow. "Our boat is called *Shangri-la.*"

"We must reciprocate your kindness," I said. "Wait a minute and I'll give you some cans of tuna—my husband caught the albacore in Mexico."

"That's great. Mom and Dad will appreciate that." And off they went.

The wine and linguini put us in a better mood. Just as we were finishing the dinner, the girls returned in the boat. This time with a chocolate log dessert swimming in raspberry sauce.

"I can't believe your generosity," I said. "We've got to meet your mom and dad."

"Come by tomorrow. We'll be here a couple of days."

We sleepily looked out the cabin windows the next morning and couldn't believe our eyes. On the stern of *Shangri-la* stood a shapely, tan blonde wearing a gold lamé bikini, cooking breakfast in an electric skillet. Not

as liberated as *Ecstasy's* queen, but certainly in keeping
with the less is best attitude.

Maurie picked up his binoculars and zeroed in on
her. "She must be scrambling eggs by the way she's
wiggling over that frying pan."

"Give me those binocs," I said. "Geez, what a figure! Is that Mama?"

"Must be," Maurie said. "I'm ready to meet Mama."
He grinned and rubbed his hands together in much
delight.

It turned out that Mama was a former airline stew-
ardess who was married to a developer from Seattle.
Thank goodness she put on a cover-up when we boarded the boat—otherwise that gold lamé would have been
terribly distracting.

Shangri-la had all the comforts of home: a large galley with a deep freeze full of gourmet food, herbs growing in pots for seasonings, a cooking counter on the
stern and a spacious salon for dining and relaxing.
Shangri-la was at least 45 feet long, twice the size of
Oops. We enjoyed a delightful visit with the family,
chattering away about our adventures in Desolation
Sound. It came time for us to depart in our dinghy back
to our boat.

"What's for dinner tonight?" Maurie asked jokingly
as we rowed away.

"Rack of lamb with rosemary," came the answer as
the cover-up was shed, revealing the gold bikini.
Maurie's eyes lit up. I don't think it was the thought of
lamb that excited him.

"We're going to pull anchor and go fishing today, but
we might return to the Harmonies tonight," he called out.

"I hope you do. We're having lime pie for dessert and we want you to have some."

The sun was scorching that day. The cabin gave us little protection from the heat as we sped along to a fishing hole near Skookumchuck Narrows. It was too hot for the fish. Maurie didn't get a bite. I tried to stay cool by periodically standing on the swim step and pouring water from the sun shower over my bathing suit.

If other women in boats have a less is best attitude, why can't I? A little skinny dip would cool me down. No boats have passed by for hours.

I wiggled out of my one piece, floral bathing suit— it looked frumpy in comparison to gold lamé. I jumped off the swim step and hit the water with a splash. It was shockingly cold. Icy tingles shot over my bare skin. When I rose to the surface, the cold took my breath away. I felt wonderfully unburdened without a suit and glided slickly through the water.

Maurie heard my splash and looked around. "Jacque, are you crazy? You'll freeze in that water. Did you go in without your suit?" He reeled in his line.

"Heck yes, everybody does it. Skinny dippin' feels soooo good. Take off your suit and come on in."

Maurie scanned the horizon for boats. He threw his old fishing hat into the cockpit and slowly untied his baggy blue bathing suit. He dove from the swim step and when he surfaced, he cried out, "Yipes, it's cold."

"I feel liberated like the queen on *Ecstasy,* don't you?"

"Christ, I'm too cold to feel liberated."

Suddenly a "whoosh" of water rose close to me. Frightened, I turned toward the sound. A black slippery creature surfaced a few feet away and looked me straight in the eye; he seemed as big as I was.

I panicked and swam toward Maurie, "Help, Maurie, there's a seal next to me. What do I do?"

Maurie laughed, "He came to visit you. Don't worry, he'll dive under."

"I don't like that critter so close." I threw my arms around Maurie's neck.

"No wonder there haven't been any fish around here—the seals scare them off, you know," Maurie said.

"I'm gettin' outta here." I thrashed in the water toward the swim step.

Maurie watched bemused. "What's the matter, Jacque, I thought you wanted to cool off and be liberated."

"Ha, not with seals nuzzling me." I reached for the slippery step ladder and started to climb out. I rose out of the water and leaned forward toward the transom. With one foot on the transom and my bottom in the air, I heard a motorboat roaring in our direction. I looked over my shoulder and saw the boat speeding closer and closer. I tried to move, but I froze in suspension, my ungracious straddling displaying parts of my anatomy that aren't exposed to much sunshine.

"Toot-toot, toot-toot," blasted the horn on the boat. And everyone waved and laughed as they passed by me.

I felt totally embarrassed. Dripping-wet, I struggled into the cockpit.

"Nothing's happened all afternoon," I called miserably to Maurie. "No fish, no boats, but as soon as we go skinny-dipping, seals and boats start making waves."

"Yep," Maurie answered, snickering as he climbed into the boat. "That was good timing, nature girl. You showed the boaters all your endowments." He grabbed a towel and wrapped it around my shivering body. "Are you trying to keep up with the girls on *Ecstasy* and *Shangri-la*?"

I gave him a coquettish look over my bare shoulder. "Um-hum." I answered and stepped inside the cabin. I heard his laughter echo across the narrows.

We returned to the Harmonies by way of Egmont Marina where we enjoyed refreshing showers. Mama and the gang greeted us, waving from the stern, as we taxied past to anchor. This time she wore a broad straw hat and a black, one-piece swim suit with a large gold anchor appliqued to point to all her girlish parts.

Maurie waved back. And let his gaze rest on Mama and her architecturally dazzling swimsuit. "This is a great place to lay anchor, don't you think?"

"Oops," I wondered, *"was that a Freudian slip?"*

22

QUE SERA, SERA

The 90's were peaceful, struggle-free years of enjoying the house all to ourselves. With Maurie semi-retired, we sometimes flew up in the fall to see the rich change of colours, to inhale the cool, crisp air. Sitting around the fireplace wearing our woolly sweaters was a refreshing change from the temperate weather of San Diego. In the spring, when Maurie went on a fishing trip, I invited a friend to Salt Spring. Flying up in a day's time made traveling to the island easy. It was a special time to idle away the hours—reading, writing, walking in the woods. Spring flowers, popping their heads from everywhere, were a delight to see.

Summertime on the island was our favourite. We drove from San Diego by way of Anacortes to pick up *Oops,* then headed for Tsawwassen to catch a ferry. Arriving on the island with little *Oops* trailing behind was always a joy. And the number of houseguests we entertained in summertime! When I leaf through our photo album, so many happy faces smile through the pages. Scenes of eating crab, picking berries, cruising on *Oops,* feasting around the dining table and relaxing on our deck bring back happy memories.

Our *Fiesta Canadiana* remained an anticipated tradition. Old friends faithfully showed up along with our new acquaintances. By the 90's, Mexican food was no longer a rarity on the island. Ganges markets displayed shelves of salsas, Mexican seasonings, cans of chilies and refried beans; tortillas, both corn and flour, lay stacked in the frozen food sections. Mexican restaurants flourished in Victoria and Vancouver. However, Maurie's touch for transforming *agave* juice to a smooth, potent *margarita* was never matched in Canada. What good times, what unexpected happenings on our Mexican night.

Like the evening Pam Wilson, a widowed friend of Carrie Louise and Cyril, attended. She was an attractive woman with stylish clothes. Pam's free spirit covered up the fact she had slow-growing thyroid cancer. Our friends Bill and Sue Bauman brought a house guest who was a widower. His deep voice greeted us as he entered through the door. "Hello, my name is Maurice Dampier, but my nickname is 'Damp.' I'm from Pasadena." Damp was a tall, broad shouldered man with a swarthy complexion and black hair. His eye caught sight of Pam. In our *casa* on that starry night, the *dos corazones* of Damp and Pam met and romance bloomed; they were married less than a year later.

One evening—after *margaritas, la comida*, dessert and coffee—there was a lull. To pep things up, I suggested to Loes, "Why don't you sing some of the songs you've learned in Mexico?" I knew she loved to sing.

"Vell, I only know two Mexican songs."

"Go ahead, let's hear them."

"Here's a really passionate love song." Loes hesitated for a moment, thought of the words, then her high melodious voice burst forth with *Flore de Pasion*. The emotion of the song caught everyone's attention. Guests slowly gathered around the dining room table to stand and listen. When she finished, everyone cheered, "More, more." Then she broke into *Que Sera Sera* and encouraged voices to join in.

"Que sera, sera," we sang, "whatever will be, will be. The future's not ours to see. Que sera, sera."

There were missing faces that night. Thea Van Meel, burdened with loneliness for Jos, sold her house and moved to Vancouver to live with her daughter Barbara. Our dear neighbour Kas Black was gone, her indomitable spirit drained by cancer. Cyril, who fought entering death's door until he was 90, was not with us.

"Now, let's all sing this favorite song together." Loes started with *I've Been Working on the Railroad.* As Loes waved her hand to conduct our singing, it was like a magic wand drawing everyone into a circle. Song after song lilted out our doors and over the harbour.

There were happy faces. Our neighbour Al Hengstler, normally quiet and reserved, beamed like a red chili as he belted out a Dixie tune, "...dem fields of cotton, dey is rotten," while he clowned around holding a kitchen broom and strumming it like a banjo. The *margaritas* were flowing in his veins. Liz Beckmann, caught up in the spirit, her Scottish eyes sparkling, danced and gyrated to the rhythm of the song. Above the din rose Jim Ballantyne's strong voice while he hammed it up on his ukulele.

Carrie Louise clapped to *Dixie,* a good ol' southern song. Her cheeks were flushed with more excitement than I'd seen in the last couple of years. The worry of watching Cyril and his death had taken its toll on Carrie.

There were serious faces too. Damp, with his deep baritone voice, captured our attention. He sang with a resolute expression on his face:

> *Someone like you*
> *A pal so good and true*
> *I'd like to leave it all behind*
> *And go and find...*

His words touched my heart, for Pam, his bride of a few years, was suffering from her recurring cancer. She stood bravely by him singing along and looking beautiful.

> *A place that's known*
> *To God alone*
> *Just a spot*
> *To call our own.*

Migs, standing next to Pam, had a solemn look in her vividly blue eyes as she sang. Wes stood behind her appearing thin and older.

Melancholy swept over the party as Damp's singing continued and we joined in:

> *We'll find perfect peace*
> *Where joys never cease*
> *Out there beneath the pale blue sky,*

Suddenly, through the night-shrouded windows I saw the missing faces. Ghosts from Mexican parties past. Cyril came into the room, merry in our floppy *sombrero,* as he loved to wear, and danced across the room. He balanced one of Maurie's *margaritas* in his hand, then lapped it up like lemonade. Through the kitchen window, Kas emerged wearing her colourful *mantilla,* carrying a tray of her delicious hors d'oeuvres which she always brought to parties. She smiled as she swirled among unseeing guests. Thea stood next to me, her beautiful eyes as big as saucers, dancing in place to the music. I felt their presence. They were with us.

> *We'll build a sweet little nest*
> *Somewhere, out in the West...*
> *And let the rest of the world go by.*

Then they were gone. I looked again at the faces in the room. Some we had known for over twenty years, others for only a short time. The atmosphere was like nothing I had ever felt at our parties. It was a moment in time, like a communion, not to be recaptured. Some eerie, inexplicable feeling overcame me. Bodies swayed together, woven closely around our table creating a human fabric that would not gather quite like this again.

A wave recedes and draws out to sea, leaving the raw shore barren, then returns, flush, frothing with power, nourishing sea life above and below the water's surface. Leaves flutter to the ground in riotous colours, fade, crumble, become earth's mulch, then tender sprouts slowly unfold to dress trees in a verdant garment. Changes of nature, changes of people, changes within personal lives, expected and unexpected, are part of life's cycle; life won't stay on hold for us, no matter how we may wish it.

And so, a generational passage took place on Salt Spring Island in the 90's. Stuart Farson, a young professor of political science and researcher for Simon Frazer University in Vancouver, bought Thea's house. He used it as a haven for writing. He doubled the size of the house to accommodate his family. We rarely saw him. Next door, the Schubart-designed house owned by Netboy, was sold to Lisa and Laurie Craig, a couple struggling to make their tow-truck business profitable on the island. The site on which the Black's trailer stood was eventually sold after Kas' death and the new owners built a "spec" home on the site.

After Cyril died, Carrie Louise was never quite the same. Left alone, somewhat isolated at the end of Long Harbour and not knowing how to drive, she seemed lost, almost helpless. Her son Allen retired from teaching a couple of years after his father's death and came to live with Carrie. Life improved for her under Allen's care. Her son had invested in island properties and was well-informed about the island's development. He exuded optimism for the future.

Pam and "Damp" Dampier, who lived next door to the Cunninghams, enjoyed five years of marriage before cancer finally took Pam. Their lovely home overlooking the harbour designed by Hank Schubart was sold.

Our San Diego friends, Harry and Barbara French, who retired on the island for eight years, sold their home on Scott Point and moved to Anacortes. The new owners built a large, sprawling addition overlooking Welbury Bay.

Another change—Wes Edwards began to lose weight and became susceptible to any bug floating by. Migs kept his diagnosis of cancer hidden until after his death in compliance with his wishes. Being a strong woman, she continued to enjoy life with island friends, her watercolour painting and traveling. She became a volunteer for the Chamber of Commerce Information Center and participated in the Art Guild. Jim and Janet, her son and daughter, had their stake in the island's future for both owned property there. Migs remained in her lovely Maracaibo home overlooking Long Harbour and the ferry terminal.

Toad Hall's days were numbered. The Beckmanns and Hank Schubart were steadily working on plans for a main house to be built on the site of Toad Hall. They had already built a stylish guest house toward the direction of Maracaibo.

For years the Beachcomber had not appeared around Scott Point. We knew his home was on his boat; we heard that he celebrated his boat's 70th year afloat. Rumor had it that he had taken several bodies from the sea and pulled innumerable boats off the rocks. Then, one day, a photograph and obituary caught my eye in the *Driftwood*.

"Maurie, look at this picture in the paper," I said.

Maurie squinted over my shoulder. "Good heavens, that's the Beachcomber. Did he die?"

"Yeah. The obit claims he did a lot of good—laying BC Hydro power line and BC Tel phone cable. The paper says, 'He was an old wharf rat.' I believe it the way he piled all that junk in the stern his boat."

I carefully laid the paper down and stared at the Beachcomber's picture. *He was one of the first islanders we met and I thought him weird. I guess he wasn't so bad after all.*

Nostalgia filled my heart. I sat back on the couch and gazed out the cathedral windows. *From the first rainy day when we moved our furniture into the house until now, so very much has happened to us.* The feeling of the passage wistfully overcame me.

We indulge in a certain vanity for our own time thinking that old neighbourhoods, old times, old friends were the very best. Not to be duplicated. Perhaps not appreciated at the time. Salt Spring was detached geographically—an island unto itself, however it was not detached from time and tide, from inevitable change. I realized our circle of friends, our experiences were undergoing that change.

"Que sera, sera."

23

TIME LINE

In the early morning, I stand on our deck to witness the day's beginning. Quiet surrounds Long Harbour. A pink sunrise glows vividly behind Nose Point. Soft breezes send our windsock waving, our Canadian and American flags fluttering. The water is dark and green and smooth. Two Canadian geese, nesting on the rocks near the fisherman's cabin, take off in tandem, their honking echoing across the harbour. In the forest, arbutus bark curls up like orange peels exposing pale-green limbs, chickadees peck on tree trunks for their breakfast and spiders arduously construct their webs between branches.

I stroll toward one special tree near the kitchen door—the surviving balsam fir tree the kids and I planted over 20 years ago. Its spreading branches have been welcoming arms to our every entry and departure. Soon, its height will tower over our house just as Scott and Charlotte as adults seem to physically tower over me. I think of how they still love to come to the island, although infrequently. I gaze at the tree. Its straight trunk reaching higher into the sky each year is a growing time-line for our years on the island.

Beneath my feet I feel the reverberation of the approaching *Queen of Nanaimo* leaving Long Harbour for its morning sail to Tsawwassen. The churning makes me wonder how many more years this ferry will sail back and forth. There's talk of eliminating the Long Harbour route and consolidating passengers at the Fulford Harbour Terminal. Won't the Fulford-Ganges Road have to be widened for more traffic? And won't there be more parking spaces needed at the Fulford Terminal? Brochures aboard the ferries show future high-speed Catamarans for longer routes and Century Class ferries for shorter, high volume routes. I sigh at the thought of more passengers and vehicles invading our island. I wave to the old queen as she slips by knowing her elegant style will never be replaced.

The ferry blasts her horn and steams out of the harbour. I sit in quiet reverie enjoying the morning. Then, in the far distance, somewhere in the sky, I hear another churning. The racket intensifies at the mouth of the harbour. Just at eye level, from our deck, I see a small float plane fly by. Its pontoons gently dip into the water spewing forth white cascades. I watch as the plane taxis down the harbour cutting a wake—its sputtering engine disturbing the quiet. Float planes have become a convenient means of fast transportation to the island for tourists, executives, professionals and boat owners. From Vancouver, it's an half hour flight. On weekends and during holidays, increasing numbers of float planes fly into Long Harbour. In Ganges, four airlines of float planes offer service from Victoria and Vancouver, bringing the island closer to civilization.

And civilization is closer. Artists, entrepreneurs and retirees have come to live among the farmers and fishermen, increasing the permanent population to 11,000+. It's a desirable place for Canadians to live, particularly for those from the east. In the summer months, tourists swell the number to 20,000, filling cottages, 100 Bed and Breakfasts and one of the few Relais and Chateau hotels in North America.

I walk inside the house to put the tea kettle on. My thoughts are interrupted by the chatter of the morning news Maurie is watching on cable television. He's happy, however, to have news from the Vancouver-Seattle T.V. stations readily available each day. While I'm waiting for the water to boil, I pick up the *Driftwood* and *The Gulf Islander,* a guide book to the Gulf Islands.

I sit outside, sip tea and browse through the *Driftwood.* A feature article on the new $24 million dollar high school appears on the front page; it states there were approximately 600 students enrolled during the last year. The paper announces all kinds of activities going on at Portlock Park; there's the summer swimming schedule at Shelby pool,   a tennis tournament being held on the four courts, athletic groups meeting at the field and track. The cinema at Central Hall advertises the showing of its two weekly movies. Big ads for savings on food dominate the paper—they come from the two supermarkets on the island. Salt Spring Golf and Country Club has its weekly blurb of winners. An article appears claiming 200,000+ tourists passed through the new Chamber of Commerce Information Center last year. The faces of innumerable realtors, ready to sell choice properties, appear in rows on full page ads. Small ads are peppered throughout the paper for art galleries, coffee houses, book stores, builders, building supplies, carpentry, etc.

I hear music. Is that bag pipe music? Yes, indeed it is. Jim's practicing again. Salt Spring has its own Royal Canadian Legion Pipe and Drum Band now and he's getting ready for a performance, I bet. I smile to myself and think of all the clubs and activities islanders participate in. There are the guilds for potters, spinners, weavers, woodworkers and painters. There's the hiking club and the sailing club and the service clubs. If Maurie and I were permanent residents on the island, we could be busy all year long.

I take another sip of tea and leaf through *The Gulf Islander.* I am amazed at the full spectrum of recreational activities featured in the booklet; hiking the scenic trails, seeing the island by bicycle, investigating marine life from kayaks, boating to provincial marine parks, camping in provincial parks, exploring the island on horseback, fishing in surrounding ocean or in the lakes, thrilling to a hang-glide trip off Mt. Bruce. The myriad of choices boggles my mind.

Where is all this progress leading? And how is the tremendous development affecting the island I so dearly love? I know the Islands Trust has been struggling to draft an Official Community Plan, known as O.C.P. The plan is supposed to set goals to protect the natural environment of the island and provide a blueprint for a new community plan. Yet, the islanders and the trustees can't seem to reach an agreement.

I think of Hank Schubart the architect who has designed more than 100 houses on the island. Since he's been on the island a long time, he's seen a lot of change. I bet he has some opinions. He's only five minutes away, down Old Scott Road, not far from our house. Maybe I'll go and ask him.

"When I saw this island, I got hooked," Hank tells me. "So in 1968, I packed my family up and moved here from San Francisco. Having a more free life without bureaucracy appealed to me Yet that's paradoxical because I believe in planning and esthetics."

"There were no bureaucracies then." I said.

"There was no C.R.D., there was no Islands Trust, there was nothing. This was an unincorporated area. When I arrived, because of the my previous experience of living in New York and San Francisco and seeing huge developments, I was concerned about what would happen to these islands. Knowing full well that development would take place in Victoria, Vancouver and Seattle, there would be inevitable consequences here. So I undertook, with a few other people, one of the first planning efforts for the whole island."

Even then Hank could foresee what might happen, I'm thinking.

"Jack Russell was on that original advisory planning committee, along with Adrian Wolf-Milner who was a surveyor and three or four others and some interesting people. This all came out of a Chamber of Commerce meeting. The big idea that governed the early planning was the concept of density zoning. Do you know about density zoning?"

"Not really."

"Jack Russell was very much involved in it. The basic idea was to take the whole land area of Salt Spring, zone it and sub-divide it in such a way that it would provide for a population 18,000 to 20,000 people. I did a further study with a friend and I'm convinced the population could grow from 26,000 to 28,000.

"Wow, that's three times what the population is now."

"Right. But then the C.R.D. took over the planning. After the Islands Trust was formed, its job was to preserve and protect the islands—that took the responsibility from the C.R.D."

"So from that," I ask, "to now, how do you feel?"

"I'm very sorry about what's happened. Very sorry. It's a question of scale. As radical as it was and hated by some, at one time there was the proposal to make an international park of the San Juan and Gulf Islands. It would have truly preserved the natural surroundings. It would have allowed people to work here and live here. That's been done very successfully in Pt. Reyes. It avoids the cutting up of the land for profit."

"But you're an architect," I say, "you've made your living through development."

"I know I'm part of the problem, but I've tried to do it as gently, as nicely as I can."

"But, there are still some rural areas here."

"It's a joke to call the island rural—it's becoming urbanized."

"Well," I say, "that's discouraging."

"It's a matter of time until the island is fully developed. With more people, more ferries and more traffic will come more conflict. The root of the problem is the long time strategies and goals of the provincial government which is in favor of development, of jobs, in favor of financial growth."

"Doesn't the amount of water available on the island control development?" I ask.

"The biggest control could be the number of ferries coming to the island. When the Islands Trust was originally formed, it was given the power to veto the ferries. That power has never been exercised. In other words, they haven't said to the provincial government, we want to protect the islands. In order to do that you have to have a long, forward-looking growth strategy. With that strategy we'll help manage population."

"Isn't the Islands Trust attempting to exercise some control through the Official Community Plan, even though the draft is still in limbo?"

"I don't want to comment on the O.C.P. I've been in planning too long and I'm too old to get involved. This I will say. The first Official Community Plan was adopted in 1974 and has been amended. But it's been allowed to go too long before changing it. Did you know the plan was to be updated every five years?"

"Oh, really. It's been over twenty, hasn't it?"

"Yes. I would rather see the trust adopt a broad series of goals that would better serve the island. Then every few years, review everything, so it's a continuing process and not a finite plan. Then the plan would be evolving and subject to change."

Driving back from Hank's, my mind is reeling. I find Maurie sitting on the deck in the cool of the afternoon, enjoying a drink and a book.

"You look bothered," he says. "What's wrong? Is it what Hank told you?"

"Yes." I tell Maurie of my conversation with Hank.

"I can see where one of the conflicts lies," Maurie says. "People who are already here with investments in the land and business don't want to lose control over how they're going to use them. They don't want the government telling them what to do. And I don't blame them. Yet, on the other hand, they want to protect and preserve the island. Esthetically people are unhappy about what's happening to the island, yet they're pleased with their financial gain. It's a universal problem."

"So, what's the solution?"

"One way would be for charitable groups or the government to buy large parcels of the land for preservation, like it's being done in the U.S.—through conservancies. Buy it at current market value."

I sigh, wondering where that kind of money would come from, and the fundamental fallacy that "buying land" represents. Better to remember the counsel of Chief Seattle: "The earth does not belong to us. We belong to the earth."

In the house, on a cabinet, sits a favourite book Mary Moat gave to us. The title is *The Elders Are Watching*. The elders are the old ones, indians living on the northwest coast years ago. The book is one poem, about 25 pages, written by teacher-author David Bouchard and illustrated by Indian artist Roy Henry Vickers. I leaf through it, marveling at Vickers' passionately bright serigraphs of eagles and raven moons. Some verses jump out at me.

> *...They want you to know they trusted you*
> *With the earth, the water, the air,*
> *With the eagle, the hawk, the raven,*
> *The salmon, the whale and the bear.*

> *...You promised you'd care for the cedar and fir,*
> *The mountains, the sea and the sky.*
> *To the Elders these things are the essence of life,*
> *Without them a people will die.*

> *...The only foe the huge forest fears*
> *Is man, not fire, nor pest.*
> *There are but a few who've come to know*
> *To appreciate nature's best.*

I put the book down and gaze through the cathedral windows at the beauty of Long Harbour as I have for twenty-five years. Twenty-five years! Just a niche of time in the thousands of years Salt Spring Island has existed. Yet years where the tide of humanity, of which we have been a part, has gradually swept over the island. I read the last lines—they're a poetic warning, *"...If the beauty around us is to live through the day, we'd better start watching...and care."*

My island memories are precious possessions. I often pull them out and reflect upon them as I have in this book. In returning to my memories, my spirit is lifted. In the returning, I can see where I have been.

Jacqueline Watson and Migs Russell Edwards.
Photo courtesy of *The Gulf Islands Driftwood.*

About the Author

Jacqueline Watson was born and raised in Anaheim, California. She studied Speech and Drama and Speech Pathology at Stanford University, earning a B.A. in Speech and Drama and M.A. in Education. Over the years, she taught part-time for the San Diego Unified School District, San Diego State University and the San Diego Community Colleges.

Upon leaving teaching, the author turned to writing. Her articles have appeared in *The San Diego Union-Tribune, The Rotarian Magazine,* the *Gulf Islands Driftwood* and the *Gulf Islands Guardian. Stuck on an Island* is her first non-fiction book.

The author lives in San Diego, California and has summered with her husband Maurice and family in their house on Salt Spring Island since 1973.

About the Illustrator

Migs Russell Edwards was born in Oakland, California. She majored in Fine Arts at the University of California and became an architectural draftsman in the San Francisco area during World War II.

She and her first husband, Jack Russell, bought property on Salt Spring Island in 1957, then moved to the island with their family in 1967. Their property became the basis for Maracaibo Estates, a strata development on the northeast side of the island.

After Mr. Russell's death, the illustrator became active in the Potters' Guild and Painters' Guild, making many contributions to ArtCraft in Mahon Hall. She was married to Wes Edwards for sixteen years before his death.